THE BIBLE:
THE BEST BITS

MARION THOMAS AND ANDREW EVERITT-STEWART

CONTENTS

FIND ME!

As you read the stories that make up a small – but important – part of the book we call the Bible, you will find some very busy illustrations.

There is something to find in every story and if you get really stuck, the answers are at the end of the book.

Look at the pictures with each story and see if you can find the details shown here.

CREATURES GREAT AND SMALL

Can you find a ladybird?

NOAH BUILDS AN ARK

Can you see two little mice?

JOSEPH, THE DREAMER

Can you count seven thin cows?

MIRIAM AND THE PRINCESS

Where is Miriam?

ESCAPE FROM EGYPT

Which man is Moses?

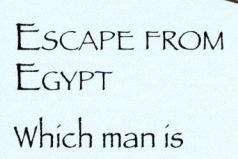

A BUSY, BUSTLING BETHLEHEM

Where is the innkeeper?

THE MAN WHO CLIMBED A TREE

Count the four birds in the tree with Zacchaeus.

DAVID AND THE GIANT

Can you find five smooth stones like this?

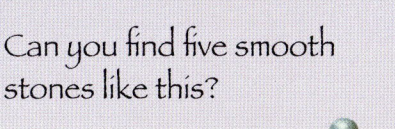

JOHN BAPTISES JESUS

Find this boy watching Jesus walk into the River Jordan.

JESUS THE KING

Can you see this boy holding a palm branch?

A CHALLENGE FOR THE PEOPLE

Can you see King Ahab?

THE HOLE IN THE ROOF

Where is the paralysed man?

A CRUEL WAY TO DIE

Find the soldier who is holding a whip.

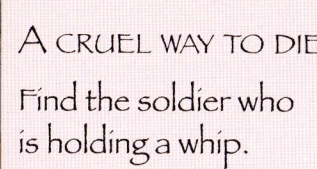

JONAH RUNS AWAY

Which one is Jonah?

CROWDS SURROUND JESUS

Where is the woman from the crowd healed by Jesus?

THE VERY GOOD NEWS!

Where is the fire that Jesus made by the lake?

DANIEL AND THE LIONS

Can you see Daniel praying to God?

MIRACLE ON THE MOUNTAIN

Find the boy who shared his lunch with Jesus.

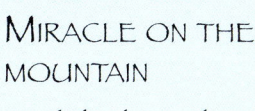

CHANGED LIVES

Can you see Peter telling people about Jesus?

CREATURES GREAT AND SMALL

In the beginning, before there was earth or sky, and before creatures of every kind lived on the earth, everything was dark.

Then God said, 'Let there be light!' and light shone in the darkness. God was so pleased that he made the land, the sea and the sky. God filled the earth with flowering plants and trees bearing fruit. He made a hot bright sun to bring light to the day and a silvery moon to brighten the dark night sky.

God filled the seas with colourful creatures and the skies with songbirds, buzzing insects and delicate butterflies.

God made animals, spotted, striped and patterned; crawling, climbing, hopping and galloping. Then God made people, a man and a woman to take care of the world he had made. God made Adam and Eve. They were his friends and they were happy.

Then God rested from the work of creation.

NOAH BUILDS AN ARK

God spoke to Noah one day.

'There is going to be a flood that will cover the whole world,' God said. 'Build an ark and fill it with all sorts of creatures so that they will be safe.'

So Noah built the ark. It was huge!

People laughed at Noah and said unkind things to him – but when it was finished, two by two, birds and animals of every kind came to him and he took them inside the ark.

Then it began to rain. For forty days and nights it rained. There was nothing to be seen anywhere but water.

After the rain had stopped and the water had gone down, the earth was clean and new and dry once more. The trees were green with new leaves. Everything smelled sweet. A bright rainbow filled the sky.

Noah, his family, and all the animals were ready to start again.

JOSEPH, THE DREAMER

Joseph had always been a dreamer. It was partly because of this that he was in Egypt instead of at home with his father Jacob and all his brothers.

But while he was in prison in Egypt, Joseph helped the king's butler and baker to understand their dreams. When the king started having strange dreams, the butler made sure Joseph was asked to help.

'God is showing you the future,' Joseph told the king. 'There will be seven years of great harvests followed by seven years with none at all. God is helping you to survive in the bad times ahead.'

So it was that Joseph the slave became a great ruler in the land of Egypt, making sure that grain was stored and no one went hungry.

The time was coming soon when he would be able to help his family too – and they would all come to live with him in Egypt.

MIRIAM AND THE PRINCESS

Miriam was pleased when she saw her new baby brother. But Miriam's mother looked worried. She knew that she had to hide her little son. The bad king of Egypt had given orders that all the baby boys born to the Israelites should be drowned!

Soon the baby was too big to hide. He cried too loudly! Miriam watched as her mother placed him in a basket by the river Nile. She waited as an Egyptian princess came to the river to bathe. She watched the princess find her little brother and heard her say she wanted to keep him.

'I will call you Moses,' the princess said.

'Shall I find someone to take care of him for you?' Miriam asked the princess. When the princess said yes, Miriam went to fetch her mother.

Now Moses was safe with the princess while his mother took care of him.

Escape from Egypt

When Moses grew up, God's people were still slaves in Egypt – and the king treated them very cruelly.

'Tell the king to let my people go!' God said to Moses. But the king would not listen. Even after nine terrible plagues of frogs and flies and biting insects – God's people were still slaves in Egypt.

Finally God sent the angel of death to pass over the homes of all God's people. But every first-born Egyptian male died that night.

'Take your people and go!' the king shouted at Moses.

They left Egypt that night with all that they owned but by the time they reached the Red Sea, they saw that the king was coming after them with his army and his best chariots.

Then God sent a strong wind to blow back the waters so the Israelites could cross safely to the other side. And God's people were free.

15

David and the Giant

David's big brothers were soldiers in King Saul's army. David was visiting them when he saw a giant of a man marching up and down and shouting very loudly. Goliath, the Philistine champion, was covered head to toe in armour and carried some fierce-looking weapons. Everyone was afraid.

'Is there a man in the king's army brave enough to fight me?' boomed Goliath.

'I will!' said David. 'God is greater than a bully like this Philistine.'

King Saul gave David his helmet but it was too big. He gave him his body armour but it was too heavy.

'God has taken care of me before,' David said. 'God will help me now.'

Then David put a stone in his shepherd's sling and aimed it at Goliath's forehead. The giant fell down dead.

A roar went up from Saul's army! David was their hero. God had taken care of him again.

A CHALLENGE FOR THE PEOPLE

For years there had been no clouds in the sky. The river beds were dry and cracked.

King Ahab worshipped gods of wood and stone instead of the God who made heaven and earth. And God had sent no rain.

'It is time to choose!' Elijah the prophet shouted to all the people. 'If the Lord is God, follow him. But if your false god is real, then follow him.'

The prophets prepared a sacrifice and prayed that their god would bring down fire to set it alight. The prophets danced and shouted, shouted and prayed. But nothing happened.

Then Elijah drenched his altar in water till it dripped.

'Lord, show everyone here that you are the true and living God,' he prayed.

Fire fell from heaven, burning the sacrifice, the wet wood and drying up the water in the trench around it. And when the people saw it, they worshipped God.

Then God again sent rain to water the earth.

JONAH RUNS AWAY

Jonah looked at the chaos around him. Sailors were clinging to the mast and trying to shout above the sound of the wind.

This was all his fault. He knew God wanted him to take a message to the Assyrians. But instead he had boarded this ship sailing in the opposite direction.

'I worship the God who made this raging sea,' he shouted. 'Throw me overboard and you will be safe.'

As soon as Jonah fell into the cold salty water, he asked God to save him. And God sent a huge fish to swallow him whole.

Jonah stayed in the body of the fish and prayed for three days. Then God caused the huge fish to spit Jonah out. This time Jonah made his way to Nineveh.

When Jonah told the people they needed to stop doing bad and terrible things, they listened and they stopped. And because he is good and kind, God forgave the people of Nineveh.

DANIEL AND THE LIONS

Daniel worshipped God even though he lived far from his home. He worked hard for King Darius in Babylon and the king trusted him.

But other men were jealous. The men plotted to get Daniel into trouble.

'Oh, king, live for ever!' they said to Darius. 'You are so great that the people should worship you. Make a law that anyone who does not should be thrown to the lions.'

Their trick worked. The law was passed.

Just as before, Daniel worshipped God and prayed three times every day. And the jealous men told the king. Darius had no choice. Daniel spent the night in the lions' den.

King Darius called to Daniel early next day.

'Here I am,' Daniel answered the king. 'God has saved me from the lions.'

King Darius knew what law he would make now.

'Daniel's God can save – even from the mouths of lions,' he said. 'Everyone must worship him.'

23

A BUSY, BUSTLING BETHLEHEM

Mary and Joseph had come to Bethlehem to be counted.

Mary was expecting her first child – a son promised to her, not in the usual way, but by an angel sent from God!

When she should have been at home in Nazareth, waiting for her baby's birth, the Roman emperor, Caesar Augustus, ordered a census – and everyone had to return to their home town.

Joseph took Mary to Bethlehem, because his family was descended from King David himself. But many others had come there too. Would there be somewhere for Mary to rest? Would there be somewhere for them to stay?

When they found there was no room at the inn, Mary made a bed for her baby son in a manger. She named him Jesus, just as the angel had told her.

25

JOHN BAPTISES JESUS

When Jesus was a man, he went down to the banks of the River Jordan. There was a man there the people called John the Baptist.

John was rather wild in appearance.

'It's time to change the way you live,' John said. 'Someone very special is coming soon. I am here to prepare the way for him. Stop doing bad things and be kind and generous instead.'

People of all ages came to be baptised in the river as a sign that God had forgiven their sins.

When John saw Jesus, he knew that the one he was waiting for had come.

'I cannot baptise you,' said John, 'it should be the other way around. I am no one!'

But Jesus persuaded John to baptise him. Then he heard God's voice saying, 'This is my son and I am proud of him today.'

THE HOLE IN THE ROOF

People had already discovered that Jesus talked about God as if he knew him well; and Jesus had the power to heal people.

Jesus was talking to a house full of people near Lake Galilee when four men came, carrying their friend on a mat. The man on the mat was paralysed and couldn't walk – but there was no more room inside the house.

The four men carried their friend up to the roof and then began to make a hole! By the time the hole was big enough to lower the man down, everyone was looking up at them.

Jesus smiled at the man on the mat. He knew why he was there.

'Stand up and pick up your mat,' Jesus said. 'You can walk home by yourself now.'

Everyone gasped when the paralysed man walked out of the house – except the four friends who knew Jesus could heal him.

CROWDS SURROUND JESUS

Crowds were ready to meet Jesus when he came across Lake Galilee. Everyone needed Jesus!

Jairus, a leader in the synagogue, was the first to ask for his help.

'Please come quickly,' he said. 'My little girl is dying!'

As Jesus made his way through the crowd he stopped suddenly.

'Who touched me?' Jesus turned and looked at the people around him.

'Look at the crowd, Master!' Peter said. 'It could have been any of them.'

But a woman came forward shyly. She had been suffering for twelve years but she had touched just the hem of Jesus' cloak – and been healed.

Suddenly someone came from Jairus' house with the news that his twelve-year-old daughter had died.

'Trust me and don't be afraid,' Jesus said.

Jesus sent everyone away except Jairus and his wife and Peter, James and John.

'Wake up, little girl,' Jesus said, taking her hand in his. Jairus' daughter opened her eyes. 'I think she's hungry,' Jesus smiled.

31

MIRACLE ON THE MOUNTAIN

Crowds followed Jesus eager to hear what he had to say about God and hoping he would heal them as they had seen others healed.

Jesus would never turn them away. Now they had followed him to a lonely place and when he had finished teaching them and healing them, his friends told him that they should be sent away. It was late and they needed to eat.

'Surely you can find food for everyone here?' asked Jesus. The disciples looked at the crowd. At least 5,000 people were there!

A boy came forward with his lunch of five small rolls and two little fish. He was happy to share it.

Jesus thanked the boy and thanked God for the food. Then he shared it with his friends. Somehow as people shared what they had with others, everyone had enough to eat. There were even twelve baskets of leftovers collected. It was a miracle!

THE MAN WHO CLIMBED A TREE

Zacchaeus lived in Jericho. He was rich – very rich. He earned his money collecting taxes for the Romans – and by keeping some of the money for himself!

When Zacchaeus heard that Jesus had come to Jericho, he wanted to see him too. But he was not the only one. Crowds lined the streets.

Zacchaeus was too short to see over the heads of the people – and no one would let him through. So he climbed into the branches of a fig tree. Now he had a better view than anyone!

But Jesus could see Zacchaeus too.

'Hello, Zacchaeus!' said Jesus. 'I thought I might come to your house today.'

Zacchaeus was a changed man when he met Jesus.

'I want to give away half of all I have to the poor,' he said. 'And if anyone thinks I have cheated them – well, I will pay them four times as much!'

Jesus smiled. 'This is why I am here,' he said.

35

JESUS THE KING

It was almost time to celebrate the Passover Feast in Jerusalem.

Jesus wanted to enter the city riding on a donkey. His friends went to collect a young colt for him from some people he knew, and then Jesus made the journey towards the city gates, riding on the donkey's back.

Some of the people in the streets already knew Jesus. They had seen the people he had healed. They had heard him talk about how much God loved them. They spread their cloaks on the ground in front of him. They waved palm branches.

'Hooray for Jesus the king!' they cheered.

'Here comes Jesus, our King!'

But there were others, religious leaders among them, who were unhappy. They didn't like the way people listened to Jesus instead of to their teaching. They began to plot together. They needed to find a way to make sure Jesus was no trouble to them any longer.

A CRUEL WAY TO DIE

The religious leaders got what they wanted.
Jesus had twelve special friends but one of them,
Judas, had decided to betray Jesus to them for
thirty pieces of silver.

Soldiers had come to arrest Jesus while he was
praying. Pontius Pilate, the Roman governor, had
questioned him. Pilate could not find Jesus guilty
of any crime. He did not want to be guilty of the
death of an innocent man…

He went to the angry crowd outside and asked
them what he should do with Jesus.

There were people in the crowd who had been
bribed by the Jewish leaders.

'Crucify him!' came the answer. 'Crucify him!'

So on a Friday morning, Pilate washed his
hands of the decision to have Jesus crucified. He
turned away as Jesus was beaten and made to
carry a huge piece of wood along the streets to a
place outside the city walls.

Then Jesus was nailed to a cross between two
criminals and left to die.

THE VERY GOOD NEWS!

Jesus had died and been buried in a borrowed tomb.

But a miracle had happened. Early on Sunday morning, some of his friends had found the tomb empty.

Mary Magdalene had met Jesus – and had seen that now he was alive! Jesus had come to see the disciples by appearing suddenly in a locked room!

Jesus was alive. There was no doubt about it. He had risen from the dead. His friends had seen him. Hundreds of people who had known him while he was with them every day had seen him.

Some days Jesus came and talked with them. On other days they waited but he did not come.

Then one night seven of the disciples went fishing. They fished all night, but by sunrise they had still caught nothing. But Jesus was there on the shore in the morning. He directed them to a huge catch of fish – and then they all had a barbecue breakfast together.

CHANGED LIVES

Jesus went back to his Father in heaven – but he had promised that he would send his Holy Spirit to be with his friends.

The Holy Spirit came to them when they were in Jerusalem. People from all over the world were there, speaking many different languages.

The disciples heard a sound like the wind. They were touched by flames of fire. Then they knew that they had the power to do anything.

'Tell God you are sorry for all the bad things you've done,' Peter told a huge crowd. 'Trust Jesus. He welcomes anyone who wants to be God's friend.'

Over 3,000 people became friends of Jesus that day. They became known as Christians. They shared everything they owned and learned to look after each other just as Jesus had taught them. And they took the message about Jesus with them when they went home, to all the people they met.

43

Did you find...?

6-7
Did you find
the ladybird?

8-9
Did you find
the mice?

10-11
Did you find
the thin cows?

12-13
Did you find
Miriam?

14-15
Did you find
Moses?

16-17
Did you find the
five smooth stones?

18-19
Did you find the king?

20-21
Did you find Jonah?

22-23
Did you find
Daniel
praying?

24-25
Did you find the innkeeper?

26-27
Did you find the boy watching Jesus?

28-29
Did you find the paralysed man?

30-31
Did you find the woman who had been healed?

32-33
Did you find the boy with the food?

34-35
Did you find the four birds?

36-37
Did you find the boy waving the palm branch?

38-39
Did you find the soldier?

40-41
Did you find the camp fire?

42-43
Did you find Peter?

First edition 2013

Copyright © 2013 Anno Domini Publishing
www.ad-publishing.com
Text copyright © 2013 Marion Thomas
Illustrations copyright © 2013 Andrew Everitt-Stewart

Published by Authentic Media Limited
52, Presely Way, Crownhill, Milton Keynes, MK8 0ES, UK.

Conforms to EN71 and AS/NZS ISO 8124

Printed and bound in China

CHALAND ANTHOLOGY #2

Freddy Lombard

HOLIDAY IN BUDAPEST / F.52

Humanoids Publishing™

HOLLIDAY IN BUDAPEST
Art: Yves Chaland
Story: Yves Chaland, Yann Lepennetier
Colors: Beaumenay – Joannet
Translation by Sasha Watson

F. 52
Art: Yves Chaland
Story: Yves Chaland, Yann Lepennetier
Colors: Beaumenay – Joannet
Translation by Sasha Watson

Graphic design: Thierry Frissen
Lettering: Jason Wahler & Thierry Frissen
Managing Editor: Paul Benjamin
Marketing Manager: Robert Silva
Circulation: Sue Hartung
Original French Version Edited by: Maximilien Chailleux
Publisher: Fabrice Giger

CHALAND ANTHOLOGY #2

Humanoids Publishing
PO Box 931658
Hollywood, CA 90093

Printed and bound in Belgium.

ISBN: 1-930652-86-0

Humanoids Publishing™ and the Humanoids Publishing logo are trademarks of:
Les Humanoïdes Associés S.A., Geneva (Switzerland)
registered in various categories and countries.
Humanoids Publishing, a division of Humanoids Group.

Freddy Lombard

HOLIDAY IN BUDAPEST

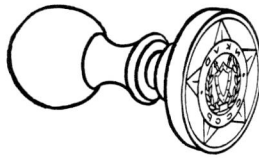

SUMMER 1956... THE HOTEL BELLA VISTA (VENEZIA). DINA IS WORKING AS A LATIN TUTOR. SWEEP AND FREDDY ARE CAMPING BY THE LAKE.

"VERCINGETORIX MINORIBUS CAESAREM ITENERIBUS SUBSEQUITUR..." ...?!?

A LETTER IN HUNGARIAN... I'M SURE IT'S NOT FROM JULIUS CAESAR. CAN YOU EXPLAIN THIS, LASZLO?

1

THE SKINNY TEENAGER NERVOUSLY SCRAWLS A NOTE FOR DINA.

PLEASE DON'T SAY ANYTHING. MY AUNT IS WATCHING US.

IT'S ALMOST 4 O'CLOCK. WE'LL CONTINUE WITH THE GALLIC WARS TOMORROW.

MISS DINA IS VERY STYLISH.

LET'S GO OUT IN THE BOAT... LASZLO, YOU'RE NOT FALLING IN LOVE WITH HER, ARE YOU?

YUCK! SHE'S A GIRL!

TELEGRAM FOR YOU, MADAME KARCSI.

IT'S FROM HUNGARY... MY GOD!

2

YOUR UNCLE WANTS US TO EXTEND OUR STAY IN ITALY. WE'LL SIGN YOU UP AT THE LOUIS-FERDINAND HIGH SCHOOL IN FLORENCE FOR THE FALL.

WE CAN'T... PAPILI, MY FRIEND LADISLAS... I WANT TO GO BACK TO THEM.

LASZLO, WE'D JUST BE ADDING TO YOUR UNCLE'S WORRIES IF WE WERE THERE NOW.

I KNOW WHAT'S HAPPENING IN BUDAPEST. STALIN'S BEEN DEAD FOR THREE YEARS NOW. PAPILI, KADAR, NAGI AND LOTS OF OTHERS HAVE BEEN SET FREE. THE "IRON CURTAIN" HAS LOOSENED ITS GRIP. NOW'S THE TIME TO KICK THE RUSSKIES OUT OF HUNGARY!

I SEE YOU'VE BEEN LEARNING A LOT IN YOUR LATIN CLASS...

PLEASE DON'T JOKE, I'M FIFTEEN YEARS OLD! AND YOU, YOU'RE JUST VACATIONING WITH ALL THESE LAZY BOURGEOIS... ALL THEY THINK ABOUT IS HAVING A GOOD TIME! YOU MAKE ME SICK!

GOOD AFTERNOON, MADAME KARCSI...

HOW NICE TO SEE YOU, COLONEL LÖWENBRÄU; HELLO FRAU LÖWENBRÄU.

HELLO, MADAME KARCSI.

LASZLO!

LASZLO'S TIRED. HE WENT TO BED WITHOUT DINNER.

I LOST CONTROL... I SHOULDN'T HAVE...

4

THAT VERY NIGHT LASZLO DECIDES TO GO HOME TO HIS UNCLE IN BUDAPEST.

DAMN, IT'S REALLY HIGH...

I... I DON'T THINK I CAN LET GO TO CATCH HOLD OF THAT BRANCH.

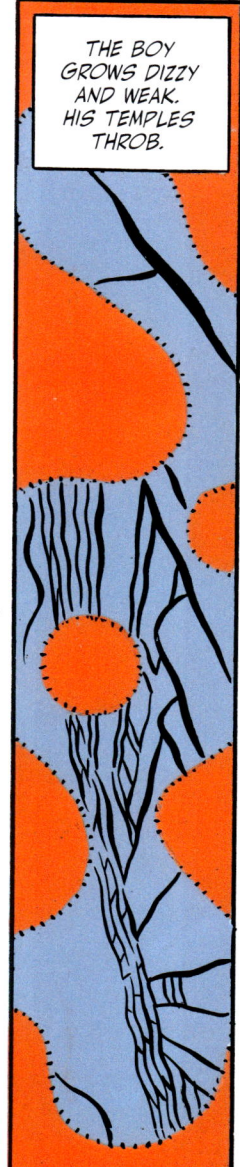

THE BOY GROWS DIZZY AND WEAK. HIS TEMPLES THROB.

OUCH! I... I LOST MY BREATH... IF I HADN'T LANDED IN THOSE BUSHES... OUCH! MY BACK! I SHOULD GET UP... I HAVE TO!

THE NEXT DAY, NEWS OF LASZLO'S DISAPPEARANCE SPREADS. THE POLICE CONDUCT A SEARCH.

MADAME KARCSI IS IN SHOCK. I GAVE HER SOME ROHYPNOL. WE HAVE TO LET HER SLEEP.

WELL THEN, PERHAPS MISS DINA MARTINO WILL ANSWER OUR QUESTIONS.

5

6

IN YUGOSLAVIA, EN ROUTE BETWEEN KRANJ AND CILLI.

HOW MUCH DOES A COLONEL IN THE HUNGARIAN ARMY EARN?

YEAH, AND HOW MUCH WILL I GET AS A CAPTAIN?

WELL, RIGHT NOW A COLONEL GETS 9,000 FORINTS BUT WHEN THE RUSSIANS LEAVE, THE ARMY WILL BE RESTRUCTURED AND...

HOW MUCH IS 9,000 FORINTS IN LIRES OR IN FRANCS?

IN FRANCS? I DON'T KNOW BUT A FORINT EQUALS HALF A DOLLAR... HMM, I HAVE PAPER AND A PENCIL IN MY BACKPACK; I'LL DO THE MATH...

HUNGARY MUST BE RICH.

RICH? NOT REALLY. MY POOR COUNTRY HAS BEEN INVADED AND PILLAGED TOO OFTEN. THE MONGOLS, THE TURKS, AND NOW THE DIRTY RUSSIANS...

BUT YOUR PARENTS ARE REALLY RICH!

I NEVER KNEW MY PARENTS. THEY WERE DEPORTED TO RUSSIA AFTER THE WAR. I WAS RAISED BY MY AUNT AND UNCLE.

MY UNCLE HAS REALLY SUFFERED TOO. HE WAS PUT IN JAIL WHEN RAKOSI, A SINISTER PUPPET FOR THE RUSSIANS, WAS IN POWER. THEY BROKE ALL HIS TEETH TO MAKE HIM ADMIT TO A CONSPIRACY THAT DIDN'T EXIST. HE WORKED IN THE MINES IN RECSK FOR THREE YEARS. THEY DIDN'T LET HIM GO UNTIL STALIN DIED. EVIL RUSSKIES! I'D LIKE TO HANG THEM WITH THEIR OWN INTESTINES!

UM... CAN YOU STOP HERE? I HAVE TO PEE.

AFFIRMATIVE, CAPTAIN.

SO, DO YOU STILL WANT TO GO TO HUNGARY?

WE PROMISED THE KID, SWEEP. BESIDES, I THINK HE'LL PITCH IN FOR THE TRIP.

LASZLO... AHEM, WE'RE GONNA HAVE TO HEAD BACK: ME AND FREDDY HAVEN'T GOT A RED CENT. BUDAPEST IS PRETTY FAR, WE'VE ONLY GOT ONE TANK OF GAS LEFT, AND I'M HUNGRY. TURN AROUND, FREDDY.

MONEY?

!

7

I HAVE 2,500 DOLLARS AND 150,000 LIRES. WE'LL CHANGE THE LIRES IN YUGOSLAVIA FOR OUR SMALL EXPENSES. WE'LL USE THE DOLLARS TO BUY WEAPONS ON THE BLACK MARKET.

THAT... WELL, THAT COMES OUT TO QUITE A FEW FLORINTS!...

LET ME SEE IT, LASZLO!

WHERE'D YOU GET THIS MONEY? I'M GUESSING IT'S NOT YOUR ALLOWANCE!

I BORROWED IT FROM MY AUNT FOR THE REVOLUTION. I'LL GET A JOB AND PAY HER BACK LATER, AFTER WE WIN.

FREDDY, I HAVE TO TAKE ANOTHER PISS. STOP THE CAR!

BUT SWEEP...

FREDDY, *PLEASE STOP!!*

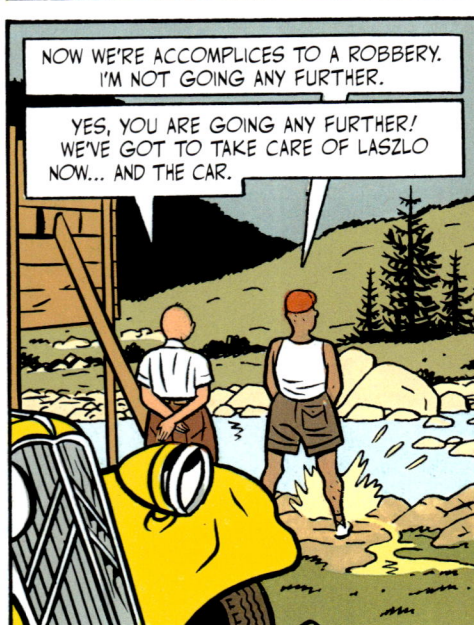

NOW WE'RE ACCOMPLICES TO A ROBBERY. I'M NOT GOING ANY FURTHER.

YES, YOU ARE GOING ANY FURTHER! WE'VE GOT TO TAKE CARE OF LASZLO NOW... AND THE CAR.

KRČMA

1,5 KM

271 B 75

SCHLAK

SCHLAK

WE'VE BEEN DRIVING A LONG TIME. IT'S ALREADY AFTERNOON. I'M HUNGRY. I'LL BUY YOU A GOOD LUNCH. FREDDY, THERE'S A RESTAURANT IN LESS THAN A KILOMETER.

HMM.

HMM.

HA! HA! HA! PASS THE BOTTLE OVER HERE, CAPTAIN SWEEP!

HERE IT IS, COLONEL LOMBARD!

KRČMA

8

10

BUDAPEST, THE WESTERN STATION. LASZLO'S AUNT ARRIVES TO MEET DINA.

HELLO, MISS MARTINO – CAN I CALL YOU DINA? – I'M IBOLYA KARCSI, THOMAS' SISTER. LET'S GO. I'LL TAKE YOUR BAGS!

DON'T WORRY ABOUT LASZLO, HE CAN TAKE CARE OF HIMSELF. TELL ME ABOUT PARIS. I WENT THERE ONCE BEFORE THE WAR. I WAS A CHILD, OBVIOUSLY. BE SURE NOT TO SPIT ON THE GROUND HERE... ... ... YES, YOU SHOULDN'T ACT POLITICAL IN THE STREETS! HEE! HEE! HEE! HEE! HEE!

DINA, DID YOU KNOW THAT ADAM AND EVE WERE COMMUNISTS? NO? AFTER ALL, THEY WERE IN PARADISE AND THEY HAD NOTHING TO WEAR! HEE! HEE!

THIS GUY MAKES HIMSELF USEFUL EVEN THOUGH HE'S DEAD... AS A SEAT FOR THE PIGEONS!

THEY SAY ONCE HE WAS GIVING ONE OF HIS SPEECHES TO THE PARTY CONGRESS AND SOMEONE SNEEZED. "WHO SNEEZED?" YELLED STALIN. WHEN NO ONE ANSWERED, HE HAD SOMEONE SHOOT THE FIRST, THE SECOND, THE THIRD ROW, UNTIL THE GUILTY PARTY CONFESSED: "IT WAS ME, COMRADE STALIN." ...

SO, STALIN GIVES A BIG SMILE AND SAYS: "BLESS YOU, COMRADE!" AND HE GOES ON WITH HIS SPEECH. HEE! HEE! HEE! FUNNY, RIGHT?... !?!?!

MY BROTHER, THOMAS, IS WAITING FOR US. WHO'S THAT? THE NEW COOK?

14

15

17

FIVE WEEKS GO BY. LASZLO STANDS HIS GROUND. HIS UNCLE KEEPS HIM LOCKED UP.

SO, COMRADE DORYPHORE, HAVE YOU DECIDED TO SUBMIT? NO? TOO BAD! GET BACK IN YOUR BOX! AH, YOU WANT TO JUMP? THAT'S TAKING THINGS A LITTLE FAR, COMRADE.

DINA! YOU DIDN'T COME YESTERDAY!

IT WAS THAT DARNED KEY! YOUR UNCLE MOVED IT... AND BESIDES, IT'S NOT EASY TO GET INTO HIS OFFICE WITHOUT HIM KNOWING!

HERE'S A LETTER FROM YOUR FRIEND STANISLAS AND A SURPRISE, THE RADIO THAT YOU'VE BEEN ASKING ME FOR.

OH! THANK YOU... YOU HAVE NO IDEA HOW BORED I AM...

IF YOU WOULD JUST BE REASONABLE, LASZLO...

WE AGREED NOT TO TALK ABOUT IT, DINA. JUST TELL ME WHAT'S GOING ON OUT THERE.

YOUR UNCLE IS WORRIED. "FREUCHE" WAS SUDDENLY CALLED BACK TO MOSCOW.

SO HE DOESN'T HAVE A SOVIET ADVISOR IN THE HOUSE ANYMORE?

DON'T GET TOO EXCITED. LOOK AT THAT TCHAÏKA, I BET THAT'S HIS REPLACEMENT GETTING HERE ALREADY.

I'M GETTING PRETTY ATTACHED TO THE KID. WE SHOULD DO SOMETHING TO HELP, EVEN THOUGH DINA DOESN'T THINK WE SHOULD. LOOK, IT'S THE NEW COOK. SHE'S A LOT BETTER LOOKING THAN OLD MARIKA. I HOPE SHE KNOWS HOW TO MAKE FRIES!

BY THE WAY, SWEEP, YOU SAY "KESIT CSOKOLOM" TO A LADY.

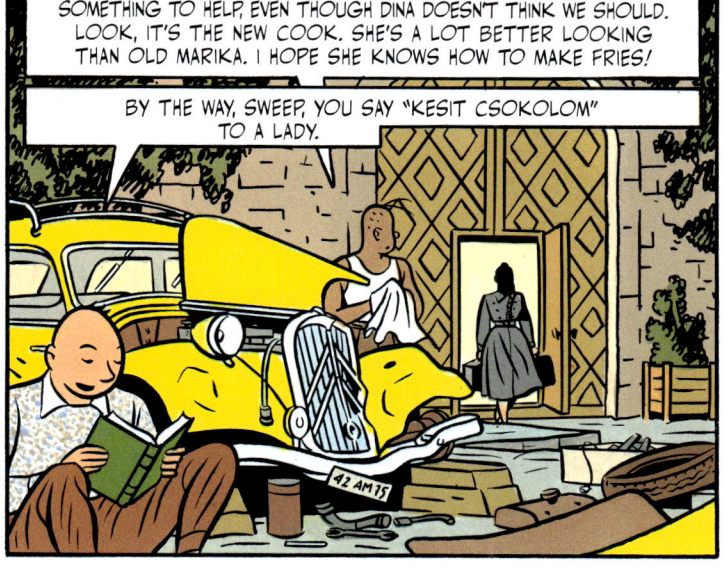

QUAISITTE CHOCOLOME, BEAUTIFUL, THE KITCHEN'S THIS WAY.

?

19

THE NEWSPAPER IS IN THE HANDS OF THE REBELS! LOOK AT THE EVENING EDITION! READ THEIR 14-POINT LIST OF DEMANDS! THEY'RE GOING TO HANG US ALL! THERE WILL BE REPRISALS, NO QUESTION! THE RUSSIANS WON'T WAIT AROUND TO HEAR THE DETAILS!

BUT THEY CAN'T MAKE ME CARRY THEIR FLAG. FERENC DOHANY WILL GO WEST AT HIS FIRST OPPORTUNITY. AT LEAST THEY DON'T CUT JOURNALISTS' THROATS THERE AND...

AND...

?

WHAT'S GOING ON?

LASZLO RAN AWAY. IT'S ALL THIS LITTLE VIPER'S FAULT!

LIAR!

LIAR? WHAT ABOUT THIS KEY? YOU STOLE IT... FROM YOUR OWN DRESSER, THOMAS!

THAT'S A SERIOUS ACCUSATION.

YES, I TOOK THE KEY! AND I TOOK IT MORE THAN ONCE! YOU HAVE NO RIGHT TO LOCK HIM UP LIKE THAT. IT'S... INHUMAN!

YOUNG LADY, I AM IN CHARGE OF LASZLO. YOU'VE BETRAYED MY TRUST!

THOMAS, THROW THEM ALL OUT. DIRTY FRENCHMEN! DECADENTS!

WHAT?! WHAT?!

YOU THINK IT'S A VACATION RESORT HERE? I'M SICK OF THIS BACKWATER! SICK OF GOULASH WITH PAPRIKA AND SICK OF THIS UGLY BAG WITH BAD CLOTHES!

SIR, I BELIEVE YOU'RE REFERRING TO MY BAG, UH... TO MY WIFE AND I'M AFRAID I MUST HAVE MISHEARD YOU.

UGLY BAG! UGLY BAG!

OOOOOOOW!

UGLY BAG!

OUCH! OUCH!

WELL, THAT ABOUT SAYS IT ALL. I THINK IT'S TIME FOR US TO TAKE OUR LEAVE. SWEEP, REMOVE YOUR INDEX AND YOUR POINTER FINGERS FROM THE GENTLEMAN'S NOSTRILS. WE'RE LEAVING!

23

24

WAIT HERE FOR ME.

FORGET ABOUT SVETLANA AND TASTE THIS DELI-CIOUS TOAST WITH PAPRIKA SPREAD.

OH! HERE'S DINA. I WAS GETTING WORRIED.

THIS IS AWFUL! LASZLO WENT TO MEET STANISLAS AT THE CORVIN CINEMA. THEY WERE PART OF A TEAM IN CHARGE OF BRINGING BACK AN AMMUNITION TRUCK FROM THE ARMS FACTORY IN CSEPEL... SOB... THEY WERE ALL CAPTURED BY THE AVO!

THE AVO?! THE POLITICAL POLICE?!

THE BAJCSY-ZSILINSKY BARRACKS IN THE AVO QUARTER.

... AND HERE'S MY STUDENT ID, AND ANOTHER ONE FROM THE CATHOLIC YOUTH GROUP, AND MY CARD FROM THE LIBRARY IN THE 10TH ARRONDISSEMENT. IT'S ON RUE DU CHÂTEAU-D'EAU IN PARIS.

REMEMBER TO BE POLITE. THEY'RE ARMED!

IN A HALF-HOUR WE'LL HAVE OUR ARMS AROUND LASZLO.

WE'LL BRING HIM BACK TO FRANCE WITH US. I'LL ADOPT THE KID IF I HAVE TO.

GREGORY!

?

LASZLO FEKETE... LASZLO HARASZTI... AH, LASZLO KARCSI, ARRESTED ON OCTOBER 25TH AT 8 P.M. IN A SCUFFLE ON BAJZA STREET. HE HAD A GUN. ARE YOU FAMILY?

HE'S ONLY 15 YEARS OLD, JUST A KID! HE WAS DRAGGED INTO THIS... YOU CAN'T HOLD HIM!

WELL, HE'S NOT HERE NOW, ANYWAY. HE WAS TRANSFERRED TO THE EASTERN STATION!

YOU'VE GOT TO SET HIM FREE!

♪ ...SET HIM FREE?... YOU'LL HAVE TO FILL OUT FORM #4706... NO, IT MUST BE THE BLUE ONE, #5206 AND...

WHAT FOR? IT MIGHT'VE BEEN THAT KID THAT SHOT YOU IN THE SHOULDER, OR THAT KILLED ZOLTAN! I THINK SIBERIAN WORK CAMP IS JUST WHAT HE DESERVES!

CALM DOWN, TIBOR! IT'S JUST A PROCEDURE. IT'S NOT FOR US TO DECIDE!

WHY DO THEY HATE US SO MUCH? WE'RE NOT SO BAD! I'M A COMMUNIST JUST LIKE ALL OF YOU!

HE'S RIGHT.

YEAH.

A THOUSAND PARDONS, COMRADE, BUT I'M NOT A COMMUNIST AND I'M AFRAID MY COMPANIONS ARE EVEN LESS SO THAN I AM.

WHAT!? SO YOU'RE FASCISTS?

NO! WE'RE FRENCH, COMRADE!

26

WHY DO THEY HATE US? I'VE NEVER TORTURED ANYONE. THEY'RE WRONG ABOUT US. WE HAVE TO CLEAR UP THIS MISUNDER-STANDING. I'M GOING TO EXPLAIN.

CIGARETTE?

YES, THANKS. YOU SHOULD SLEEP NOW WHILE IT'S CALM.

YOU'RE THINK-ING ABOUT YOUR FRIEND, LASZLO.

I'M WORRIED.

WELL DON'T BE. IT'LL WORK OUT. WE'LL ALL UNDERSTAND ONE ANOTHER EVENTUALLY, YOU'LL SEE. WAIT FOR ME HERE.

GREGORY, WAKE UP! TIBOR'S IN THE COURTYARD WITH A WHITE FLAG!

I WANT TO TALK! DON'T SHOOT!

I'M HUNGARIAN, JUST LIKE YOU. I WAS BORN IN THE NORTH, IN SÁROSPATAK.

I HAVE PARENTS AND FRIENDS THERE. ANYONE WHO KNOWS ME WILL TELL YOU, I'M NOT SUCH A BAD GU...

BRATABR ATABRAT

28

AT NIGHTFALL THE FIGHTING STARTS AGAIN.

THIS IS IT! THEY'RE GOING TO LYNCH US! THE PARTY'S ABANDONED US!

THE PARTY WOULD NEVER BETRAY US! COMMANDER KONOK SAID THE RUSSIAN TANKS ARE COMING!

LASZLO... KARCSY, BORN... MARCH 30TH... 1941... IN BUDAPEST...

DING!

HERE'S THE FORM YOU HAVE TO FILL OUT. IT'S GOT THE SIX OFFICIAL STAMPS ON IT. GIVE ME THE JACKET.

OKAY

GREAT! NICE CUT! "RENÉ DUPONT" "PARIS" WHAT STYLE!

HEY... THIS PAPER ISN'T SIGNED!

ONLY COMMANDER KONOK CAN DO THAT. IT WON'T COST YOU ANYTHING TO ASK HIM. HE'S ON THE 4TH FLOOR, OFFICE # 419.

THIS IS COMRADE KONOK SPEAKING! WHAT'S IT ABOUT? THE BARRACKS AT BAJCSY-ZSILINSKY ARE GOING TO FALL! WE DON'T HAVE ANY AMMUNITION LEFT! THE REBELS ARE MAKING THEIR FINAL ATTACK!... WHAT?... HE'S BUSY? WHAT COULD BE MORE IMPORTANT? THIS IS A MATTER OF LIFE AND DEATH!

THESE BLASTED POLITICIANS! THEY SACRIFICE US WITHOUT BLINKING! WE SHOULD'VE KILLED THEM ALL IN THE MINES IN GOROD. THERE'S ONLY ONE THING LEFT TO DO... BUT NOT WITH A GOVERNMENT WEAPON!

AT LEAST YOU WERE FAITHFUL TO THE END, OLD FRIEND!

29

30

31

WHAT ARE YOU WAITING FOR? WE'VE GOT MORE IN LINE.

THEY SAY THEY'RE FRENCH.

HER? THAT SLUT? I RECOGNIZE HER, SHE'S COMMANDER KONOK'S SECRETARY!

NO, SHE'S NOBODY'S SECRETARY! WE'RE FROM PARIS, FRANCE, CHARLES TRENET...

SWEE-EET FRA-ANCE, DEAR COUNTRY OF MY CHI-ILDHOOD...

HOLD ON, FREDDY, I'VE GOT PROOF.

LOOK, MADE IN FRANCE! DO THE AVO WEAR SHOES LIKE THESE?

THAT DOESN'T PROVE ANYTHING. WE JUST SHOT SOMEONE WEARING A CHECKERED JACKET FROM PARIS.

STANISLAS!

DINA!

WHERE'S LASZLO?

I GOT LUCKY AND ESCAPED BY JUMPING OUT OF THE TRUCK... THE RUSSIANS ARE HOLDING HIM PRISONER AT THE EASTERN STATION.

DINA!

THEY'RE GONNA SHOOT US!

SWEE-EET FRANCE

OUCH

ARE THOSE YOUR FRIENDS? I'LL TAKE CARE OF IT.

WITH THE HELP OF COLONEL LAKATOS, STANISLAS QUICKLY RESOLVES THE PROBLEM.

32

STANISLAS' GROUP OCCUPIES THE SANDOR BRODI SCHOOL. THE YOUNG MEN WATCH OVER THE NEIGHBORING STREETS.

THE T-34 TURRET WAS OPEN. I WENT FOR IT! FERI COVERING ME, OF COURSE. I CLIMBED THE TANK AND THEN THREW MY "BOTTLE." YOU SHOULD'VE SEEN IT, PETER! I BARELY HAD TIME TO GET AWAY. MY FIRST TANK! IT WAS INCREDIBLE!

HA HA!

CONGRATS!

IT MIGHT'VE BEEN INCREDIBLE BUT YOU LEFT YOUR POSITION AND ABANDONED YOUR COMRADES. WE HAVE TO BE DISCIPLINED. THE RUSSIANS AND THE AVO DON'T JOKE...

SHHH! I'VE GOT RADIO KOSSUTH!

THE PRESIDENT OF THE PATRIOTIC POPULAR FRONT, IMRE NAGY, HAS AGREED WITH THE SOVIET GOVERNMENT TO A TOTAL AND IMMEDIATE WITHDRAWAL OF THE RUSSIAN TROOPS STATIONED IN HUNGARIAN TERRITORY AND HE ORDERS A GENERAL CEASE-FIRE.

OH!

HURRAY! HURRAY!

THE YOUNG MEN SING THE MARSEILLAISE IN FRENCH...

WE AGAINST ALL TYRANNY...

SHHH! THERE'S MORE!

...COMRADE THOMAS KARCSI, HAS BEEN NAMED TO THE NEW NAGY GOVERNMENT.

HUNH?

WONDERFUL!

THAT'S LASZLO'S UNCLE!

HEY, STANISLAS, SHOULD WE TURN IN OUR WEAPONS?

WE WON!

I WOULD'VE GOTTEN A TANK!

I DON'T TRUST THE RUSSIANS. YOU COULD SKIN THEM AND FRY THEM UP IN BUTTER AND THEY'D STILL BE DIRTY RUSSIANS!

33

AND LASZLO?

BUT THIS LIBERATION ORDER ISN'T VALID FOR THE RUSSIAN NKVD. I THINK WE'LL HAVE TO WAIT FOR THE NEGOTIATIONS TO BE OVER...

NEGOTIATIONS? YOU'RE SO NAÏVE! I'M KEEPING MY GUN! AS FOR THE PRISONERS IN THE EASTERN STATION, THEY'LL BE DEPORTED LIKE THE OTHERS!

LACI IS RIGHT. WE STILL HAVE TO BE CAREFUL.

WE NEED THAT STAMP! SWEEP, YOU'LL GO IN ALONE. THIS TIME, INSTEAD OF FORCE, YOU'LL USE YOUR SEX APPEAL.

WHAT?! SVETLANA VLATIVOLOVA? BUT...

"MEETING PLACE, BAROS SQUARE, WITH THE PAPER WE NEED STAMPED."... FREDDY COMES UP WITH SOME GOOD ONES. WHEN I KNEW SVETLANA SHE WAS JUST A SIMPLE COOK TO ME...

AND NOW I'M TERRIFIED!

YOU'RE FRENCH FROM FRANCE? COME HAVE A GLASS OF FREUCHE WITH US TO CELEBRATE!

AH, JUST A GLASS. EVEN FREDDY COULDN'T REFUSE.

LONG LIVE CAMUS! LONG LIVE SARTRE!

NOW, HIC, I'VE GOT TO GO.

NO! WE'LL DRINK TO THE HEALTH OF MISTINGUETT AND THEN TO MARCEL CERDAN!

STAY AND SING US A SONG, YOU DIRTY RUSSIAN!

A ♪ BELL RINGS RINGS ♪ IT'S FOR JEAN FRANÇOIS ♫ NICO...

YOU'RE IN MY WAY! HIC!

HEE! HEE! HE'S GETTING MAD...

HERE'S ONE FOR SARTRE!

ETIENNE!

GUG

AND HERE'S ONE FOR MISTINGUETT!

ATTILA!

MOF

34

AH, MY FRENCH CHIVALRY KEPT ME FROM HITTING A PERSON OF THE FAIR SEX, HIC, MY RESPECTS, MADAME! HA! HA HA!

BRATABR

HIC!

WHAT'S GOING ON, SWEEP? YOU KNOCK OUT HUNGARIANS LIKE ANOTHER GUY BREAKS MATCHES BUT YOU WILT AS SOON AS YOU THINK OF SVETLANA... WHAT'S WRONG, OLD BOY?

HERE WE GO! COMRADE THOMAS KARCSI'S PAYING A VISIT.

THIS IS ALL WRONG, MATYAS! YOU CAN'T INCLUDE ME IN YOUR NEW GOVERNMENT WITHOUT MY CONSENT!

SO YOU'RE NOT WITH US, THOMAS?

ALL YOU CAN THINK ABOUT ARE THE RUSSIANS AND THEIR ENDLESS NEGOTIATIONS. MEANWHILE THEIR TANKS ARE SURROUNDING BUDAPEST. THE REBELLION IS OVER!

IF YOU'RE NOT WITH US, YOU'RE AGAINST US!

NO! YOU'RE CRAZY! OUR REVOLUTION HAS TO STAY PURE! LET'S GO! GOODBYE, THOMAS!

I WOULD HAVE BLOWN HIS BRAINS OUT IF HE'D FIRED!

AND WE'D HAVE LEFT THREE MORE CORPSES. NOT THAT IT WOULD'VE MATTERED MUCH...

LASZLO IS DEAD... THE FUTURE IS MEANINGLESS. BUT I HAVE TO GO ON LIKE BEFORE... INTO AND AGAINST IT ALL.

THE PLANE TAKES OFF AT 10 O'CLOCK. A CAR WILL PICK US UP. BE READY. TOMORROW NIGHT WE'LL BE IN MOSCOW.

ALL THIS NERVOUS TENSION IS WEARING ME OUT...

I'D TAKE A HORSE OVER THESE DAMN PEOPLE ANY DAY, ONE OF THOSE PURE BLOODED WILD STALLIONS I USED TO RIDE WHEN I WAS TWELVE...

WHERE ARE MY LOVELY YOUNG CHEEKS OF BYGONE DAYS?

I NEED SOME EXERCISE, TO BE WHIPPED BY THE FRESH AIR OF THE STEPPE.

OUCH!

UGH!

HAN!

36

SWEEP!
MY CAUCASIAN STALLION!

YOU RISKED EVERYTHING TO FIND ME AGAIN! OH, BUT YOU'RE HURT!

I'LL BRING YOU A COLD COMPRESS.

YOU MUST BE BURNING UP IN THAT COAT...

MMMH... I'M TREMBLING... (SIGH)

HOW DO YOU FEEL?

I HAVE TO GET HER TO LEAVE ME ALONE.

OOH! MY HEAD HURTS. COULD I HAVE AN ASPIRIN?

37

DID YOU REALLY COME BACK TO SEE ME, SWEEP?

OH, ALL AT NOT, I... I WANTED JUST A STAMP, UH, TO KISS YOU, BEFORE LEAVE I GO!

LOOSENED BY SWEEP'S NERVOUS TREMBLING, THE DOCUMENT, HASTILY STUFFED INTO HIS SHORTS, FALLS TO THE GROUND.

?

OH NO! I'M A DEAD MAN!

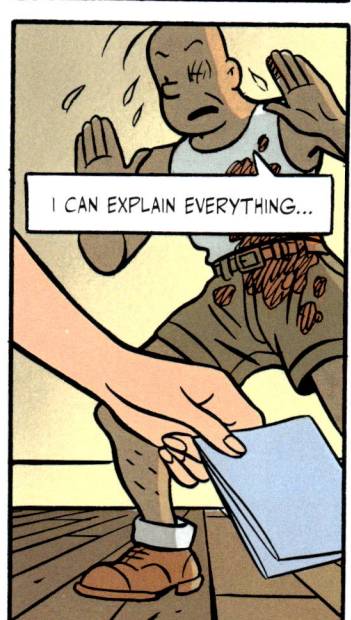

I CAN EXPLAIN EVERYTHING...

A SCOWL DARKENS SVETLANA VLATIVOLOVA'S FACE.

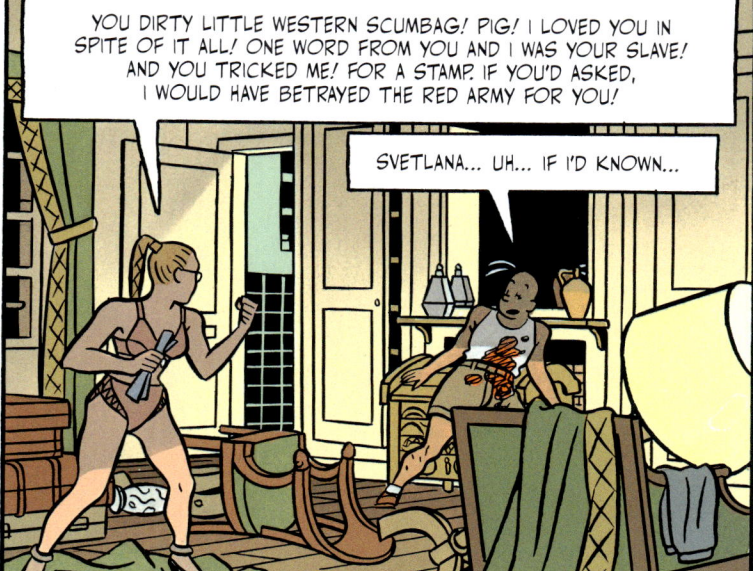

YOU DIRTY LITTLE WESTERN SCUMBAG! PIG! I LOVED YOU IN SPITE OF IT ALL! ONE WORD FROM YOU AND I WAS YOUR SLAVE! AND YOU TRICKED ME! FOR A STAMP. IF YOU'D ASKED, I WOULD HAVE BETRAYED THE RED ARMY FOR YOU!

SVETLANA... UH... IF I'D KNOWN...

NOW YOU'LL GET NOTHING! NO SVETLANA, NO RED ARMY, NOT EVEN THIS MISERABLE SCRAP OF PAPER!

I LOVED YOU TOO, SVETLANA.

39

WHY WASN'T I HONEST? WHY DID I LIE? IF IT HADN'T BEEN FOR THAT PAPER... ALL THIS FOR THAT MULE-HEADED LASZLO... IT'S TRUE, I WAS MEAN TO HIM...

BUT IF WE'D JUST STAYED IN ITALY AND CAMPED OUT... YES, IT'S REALLY ALL FREDDY'S FAULT THAT I LOST SVETLANA'S HEART. THEY SHOOT AT PEOPLE FOR NO REASON HERE, BUT I'VE GOT A THOUSAND REASONS TO KILL FREDDY.

WHY DO I PUT UP WITH HIM? THAT'S THE REAL MYSTERY! BECAUSE I ALWAYS END UP FORGIVING HIM. AND THEN HE DOES IT AGAIN, AND I SUFFER AGAIN.

DURING THE NIGHT, THE THOUSANDS OF RUSSIAN TANKS GATHERED AROUND BUDAPEST INVADE THE HUNGARIAN CAPITAL. AT THE SAME TIME, THE PRINCIPAL LEADERS OF THE REBELLION ARE ARRESTED. AMONG THE FREEDOM FIGHTERS, CONFUSION GIVES WAY TO PANIC. SOME FLEE TO THE WEST. OTHERS, PREFERRING DEATH TO SLAVERY, CONTINUE FIGHTING WITH THE STRENGTH OF DESPERATION. GROUPS OF PRISONERS GATHER AT THE EASTERN STATION BEFORE BEING DEPORTED TO RUSSIA.

40

41

42

43

GET OUT OF HERE! WHAT DO YOU HOPE TO GAIN BY STAYING? TO MAKE UP FOR YOUR UNCLE'S BETRAYAL? IT'S TOO LATE! SAVE YOUR HIDE, BRAT!

LEAVE ME ALONE JÓCZI, IT'S NONE OF YOUR BUSINESS.

LAST CALL FOR COMRADE LASZLO KARCSI...

LISTEN TO ME, ALL OF YOU. I AM JOSZEF ASTÁLOS AND I KNEW YOUR UNCLE WELL, LASZLO.

WOW, IT'S THE OLD PEASANT POET, THE ONE WE STUDIED IN SCHOOL.

?

MAYBE YOU WERE RIGHT. YES, I REMEMBER NOW! THEY REPLACED CONVOY 83 WITH 82. SO HE LEFT LAST NIGHT.

SEE, YOU SHOULD LISTEN TO ME.

YOU HAVE NOTHING TO BE ASHAMED OF, LASZLO, YOUR UNCLE IS A BRAVE MAN, A HUNGARIAN WHO PUTS HIS COUNTRY ABOVE ALL ELSE.

BUT HE BETRAYED THE REVOLUTION!

IT'S TRUE, HE BEARS THAT WEIGHT, BUT HE DID IT FOR HIS COUNTRY. THE REVOLUTION WAS A GOOD CAUSE, BUT, ALAS, IT WAS A LOST CAUSE. YOUR UNCLE UNDERSTOOD THAT FROM THE BEGINNING.

POLITICS IS LIKE A GAME OF CHESS. YOU HAVE TO KNOW HOW TO SACRIFICE PIECES IN ORDER TO WIN. TODAY, HUNGARY'S FATE LIES IN THE HANDS OF MEN LIKE YOUR UNCLE. MAY GOD KEEP HIM AND LET HIM WATCH OVER OUR COUNTRY.

SO IF CONVOY #83 REPLACED CONVOY #82, IF IT WASN'T SABOTAGED AGAIN, IT WOULD HAVE CROSSED THE BORDER THIS MORNING AT 6:22 TO ARRIVE IN SIBERIA. LET'S MAKE SURE I'M NOT MISTAKEN... WITH THE TIME CHANGE...

44

JUMP, IBOLYA DARLING.

GET CLOSER, YOU IDIOT! DO YOU WANT ME TO FALL?

THIS WAY! THERE ARE BLANKETS AND MILK.

IF YOUR FRIEND, THIS... THIS FREDDY, HADN'T BEATEN THE AVO BORDER GUARD, WE'D ALL HAVE BEEN KILLED.

MY NOVEL WILL BE CALLED "HUNGARY, THE MARTYR." NO, NO, "I WAS A REBEL FIGHTER." THAT'S GOOD!

STAY STILL!

YOU CAN BUY ME BEAUTIFUL DRESSES WITH YOUR ROYALTIES. I'LL HAVE NAIL POLISH AND LIPSTICK.

HOW WONDERFUL! YOU'LL LOOK JUST LIKE A PRINCESS.

I KNOW HOW YOU FEEL, LASZLO. WE ALL LEFT SOMETHING IMPORTANT BACK THERE.

FOR ONCE, WE AGREE. IT WAS A GOOD CAR.

45

Freddy Lombard

F.52

THE BOURGET AIRPORT

ZONE RESERVEE
Accès interdit

F-5

YOU KNOW, JOJO, MY FATHER BUILT THE F-52.

YEAH, RIGHT! YOUR FATHER'S JUST A WORKER IN THE CHÂTILLON FACTORY. MINE WORKS AT THE FRANCO-AMERICAN BANK. THEY FINANCED THE PROJECT.

HEY, WHEN'S THE PLANE GONNA TAKE OFF, JOJO?

...WELL, DEAR LISTENERS, IN JUST 40 MINUTES WE WILL WITNESS THE LIVE TAKEOFF OF THE F-52, THE FIRST ATOMICALLY POWERED COURIER PLANE. WITH THIS INAUGURAL NON-STOP FLIGHT FROM PARIS TO MELBOURNE, A PAGE IN HISTORY IS TURNED. A PAGE? NO, WE'RE WRITING A WHOLE NEW CHAPTER IN HUMAN HISTORY TODAY, DEAR LISTENERS... AND THE CREW LOOKS READY TO BOARD...

WE'RE MISSING THE THREE PEOPLE WE HIRED YESTERDAY.

1

2

LIVE FROM BOURGET, DEAR LISTENERS, FOR THE MOST IMPORTANT EVENT SINCE CHARLES LINDBERGH'S LANDING 25 YEARS AGO...

NON-STOP FROM PARIS TO MELBOURNE IN LESS THAN 24 HOURS. THE PLANET'S GETTING SMALLER EVERY DAY. I'D LIKE YOU TO HEAR THE THOUGHTS OF A FEW OF THE PASSENGERS, EACH ONE A MODERN-DAY ICARUS. THEY'LL BE TAKING OFF JUST MOMENTS FROM NOW...

HA! DON'T WORRY, THESE THINGS ARE ALWAYS LATE! I WAS AT ALL THE BIG TAKE-OFFS. SANTOS DUMONT, NUGESSER AND COLI. MERMOZ WOULD ALWAYS TELL ME, "THE MAIL COMES FIRST." BUT THEY NEVER SAID EXACTLY WHAT TIME IT WOULD COME... IT CAME WHEN IT CAME! HA HA HA!

BESIDES, THEY WON'T LEAVE WITHOUT THE MAILBAGS!! 350 KILOGRAMS OF LETTERS, ALL WITH COMMEMORATIVE STAMPS. HA! THEY'D SURE BE VALUABLE IF THERE WERE AN ACCIDENT...

IT'S WONDERFUL. THE AIRLINE IS OFFERING AN INCREDIBLE DEAL FOR LARGE FAMILIES. THE ONLY PROBLEM IS THAT WE'LL BE GOING SO FAST, WE WON'T HAVE TIME TO LOOK AT THE COUNTRYSIDE.

1000 KM / HR. IS THIS THE FASTEST HUMANS WILL EVER TRAVEL?

WELL, I HOPE NOT, AIRPLANE TRIPS ARE SO LONG AND MONOTONOUS....

YES, SO BORING!

AND YOU, SIR, ARE YOU TRAVELING IN LUXURY CLASS OR ECONOMY?

GRRR...

HMM, NOT A TALKER.

AND YOU, MY DEAR? READY TO CLIMB INSIDE THAT BIG STEEL BIRD?

I'M GOING TO SEE THE KANGAROOS WITH MY RABBIT AND MY MOMMY.

OF COURSE, YOU'D STILL HAVE TO FIND THE MAIL IN THE WRECKAGE. THIS ONE TIME...

3

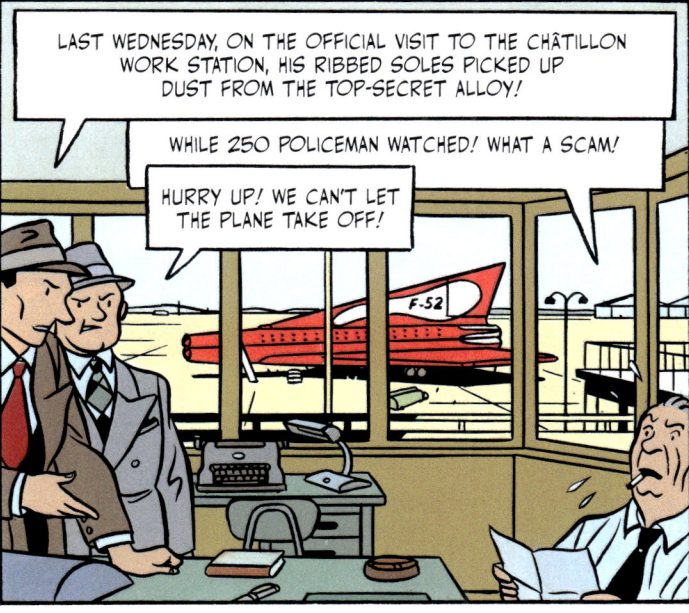

THAT'S ENOUGH! STOP CRYING AND READ YOUR BOOK! I'LL BUY YOU ANOTHER DOLL IN MELBOURNE...

IS DADDY COMING WITH US?

YES, SWEETIE, YOUR DADDY'S IN HEAVEN WATCHING OVER US WHEREVER WE GO!

CÉLINE SAYS DEAD PEOPLE JUST GET BURIED AND THEY DON'T GO TO HEAVEN.

CÉLINE DOESN'T KNOW WHAT SHE'S TALKING ABOUT.

IS HE ALWAYS GOING TO BE IN HEAVEN? BECAUSE I WANT HIM TO COME PLAY WITH ME, AND TO TELL CÉLINE THAT SHE'S DUMB.

MOMMY, I SAW DADDY, YOU KNOW. HE WENT INTO FIRST CLASS TO GET MY RABBIT FOR ME.

SO, YOU SEE, IT'S ALL WORKING OUT OKAY...

I HAVE TO PEE.

BE CAREFUL AND WASH YOUR HANDS.

WHAT A LITTLE HANDFUL...

7

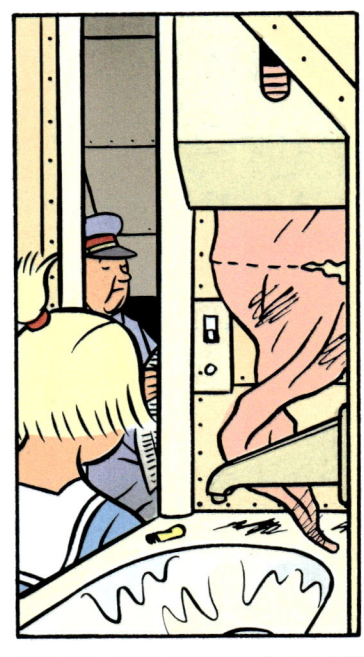

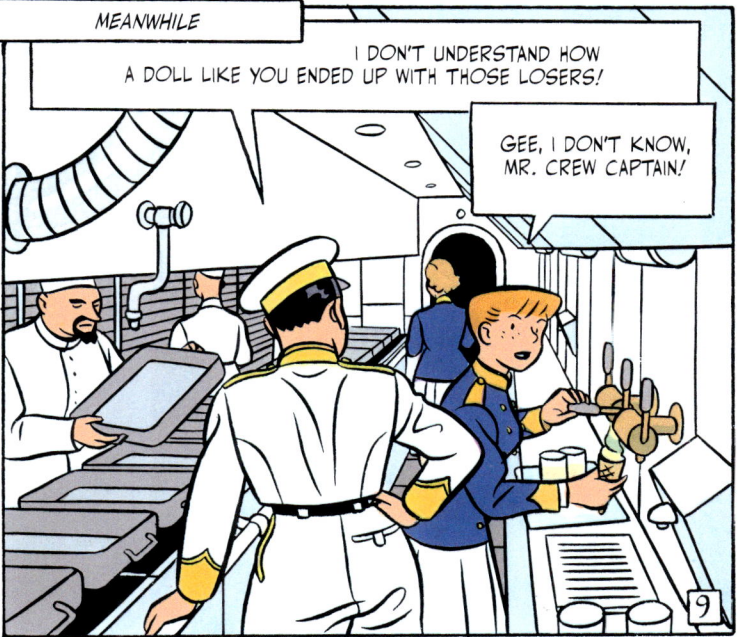

9

MEANWHILE.

WHAT'S ISADORA DOING? SHE MUST HAVE FOUND A FRIEND.

OUCH!

FLOP

OH, YOU BRATS! LET'S SEE WHAT YOUR PARENTS HAVE TO SAY ABOUT THIS

HAW HAW!

YOU AGAIN! MISS, I JUST HOPE YOU NEVER HAVE CHILDREN!

I HAVE A DAUGHTER, MA'AM, AND...

WELL, I FEEL SORRY FOR HER! YOU PROBABLY YELL AT HER ALL THE TIME. SHE'LL END UP NEUROTIC!

WE WANT TO NEUTRALIZE THE SPY WITHOUT CALLING ATTENTION TO HIM. WE'LL HAVE TO INSPECT ALL OF THE PASSENGERS' SHOES. LET THE FLIGHT ATTENDANTS KNOW...

AT YOUR SERVICE, SUPERINTENDENT!

COMMISSAIRE DE BORD

ANOTHER VODKA, PLEASE.

DING

OH! THE TELEPHONE!

Davidoff

FIRST CLASS BARTENDER, FREDDY LOMBARD AT YOUR SERVICE... HUNH? A RUSSIAN SPY... HIS SHOES? OKAY! I'LL BE DISCREET!

SOME STORY!

YOUR VODKA, SIR...

OH, HE'S GONE.

19

13

14

CABIN 21

GOOD JOB, SHEILA! YOU WERE REALLY BRAVE. THE STEWARDESS DIDN'T EVEN NOTICE. HEE HEE HEE! THIS IS FUN.

AAARH! AAAARH!

DO YOU WANT TO GO SEE MOMMY? I BET SHE WON'T BE ABLE TO TELL US APART!

WAIT, ISADORA, TRY ON THESE GLASSES!

HA! HA!

YOU CAN'T TELL THEM APART!

HA HA HA! HA HA HA!

OOH! I'M DIZZY!

CRK

NOW THAT'S THE RIGHT PRESCRIPTION!

MEANWHILE

HAVE YOU SEEN MY DAUGHTER? ISADORA? SHE'S FIVE YEARS OLD... SHE'S WEARING A BLUE DRESS.

NO, MA'AM.

afé 5 FRS

SHE WENT TO THE BATHROOM A HALF-HOUR AGO.

NO, I HAVEN'T NOTICED HER.. HAVE YOU, GEORGE? OH, YOU NEVER NOTICE ANYTHING!

UH...

I'M WORRIED. I'VE CHECKED THE CABIN TWICE AND... COULD SHE HAVE GONE UP TO FIRST CLASS?...

15

16

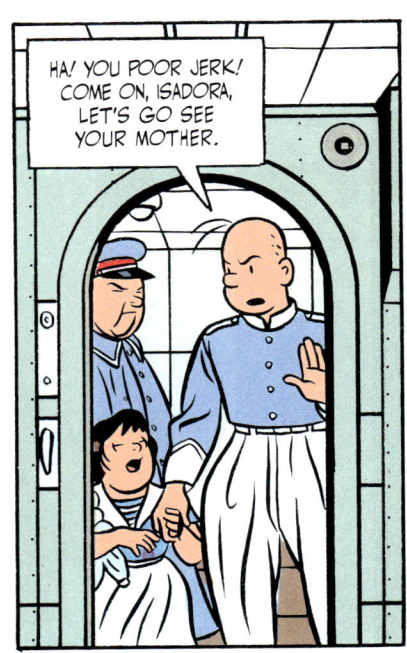

18

19

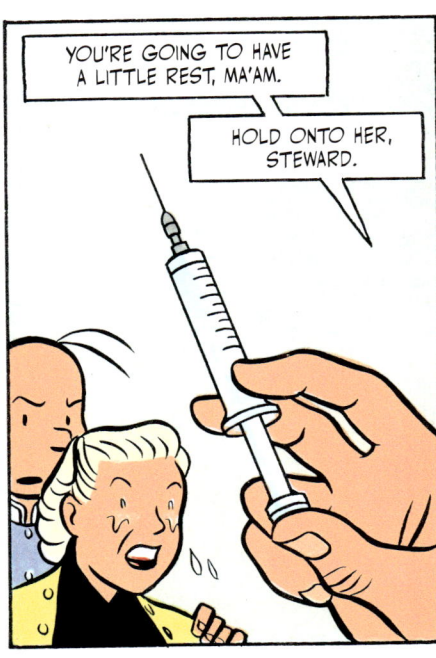

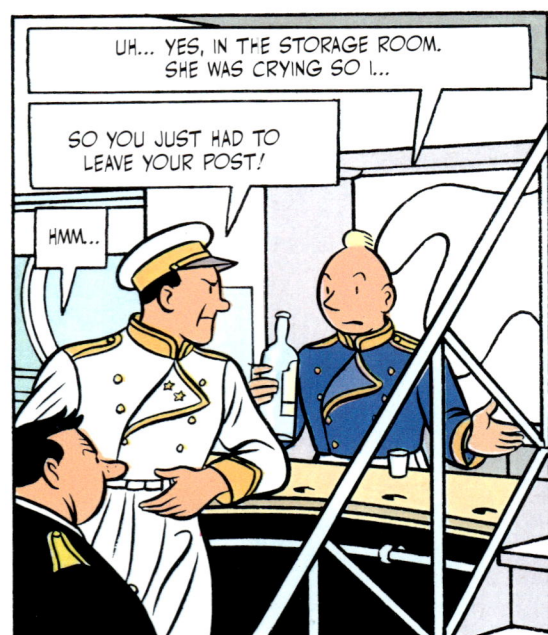

20

21

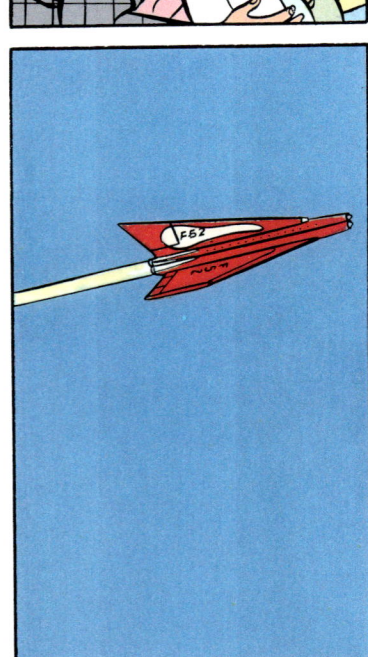

22

EXCUSE ME, SIR, BUT EVERYONE HAS TO PARTICIPATE. NO SPOILSPORTS!

OKAY, OKAY.

HA HA! HE HAS HOLES IN HIS SOCKS!

THANK YOU, SIR, AND GOOD LUCK!

MEANWHILE, IN LUXURY CLASS.

EVERY HOUR THAT GOES BY IS ANOTHER HOUR OF FREEDOM!

LATER...

THE SHOES SAY IT ALL. OUR SPY ISN'T IN ECONOMY CLASS.

BLAST IT! THIS IS TOUGH. WE'LL HAVE TO EXTEND THE OPERATION TO FIRST CLASS.

THIS TIME, ACT ALONE AND BE CAREFUL. PLAY IT SMOOTH! YOU'RE RESPONSIBLE FOR THE REPUTATION OF THE F-52 AND THE ENTIRE COMPANY!

GOT IT. NO MISTAKES!

GO GIVE THE SHOES BACK TO THEIR OWNERS. I'M ON AN IMPORTANT MISSION.

YOU WANT ME TO... GIVE BACK... OH... OKAY!

... AND WHAT ABOUT THE PERISHABLE STOCKS?

WHAT I DO IS, I SEND THAT STUFF TO LATIN AMERICA THROUGH A COUPLE OF HUMANITARIAN AID GROUPS...

SMOOTH... PLAY IT SMOOTH...

EXCUSE ME, GENTLEMEN, BUT YOUR SHOES LOOK A LITTLE DUSTY. MAY I TAKE THEM TO BE POLISHED?

?

?

23

24

CAN I TRADE YOU A PAIR OF HIGH HEEL IMITATION SNAKESKIN PUMPS FOR A PAIR OF SIZE 39 LOAFERS?

WHO WON?

OH... WELL, THE CREW IS STILL THINKING IT OVER.

THESE AREN'T MY SHOES!

I HAVE TWO LEFT FEET.

SHE'S STILL SLEEPING. I'LL PUT HER SHOES BACK ON WITHOUT WAKING HER.

SHE SEEMS LIKE A NICE LADY. TOO BAD SHE'S OFF HER ROCKER!

AND THAT LITTLE GIRL WILL END UP IN AN INSTITUTION. IT'S SAD...

PLEASE, SIR, LISTEN TO ME.

UH OH! I HOPE SHE'S NOT GOING TO GO NUTS ON ME!

26

27

ALL THE KIDS UPSTAIRS ARE AT THE PUPPET SHOW AND DINA'S WATCHING THEM. I'LL BET SHE CAN HELP ME...

52

52

HA HA! WE'LL SHOW THAT BRUTUS!

SCOUNDREL! I'LL GET YOU, CREEP!

WATCH OUT, GUIGNOL!

CAREFUL!

CATCH ME IF YOU CAN, IDIOT!

HA! HA!

ALL THE POLITICAL CONTENT IS SUPPRESSED IN FAVOR OF A MANICHEAN DISPLAY WITH ABSOLUTELY NO SATIRICAL EDGE...

SHHH, GO BACK TO YOUR SEAT!

GNAFRON, HELP ME!

BANG BANG OUCH OUCH!

?

SHHH!

SWEEP?!

YOU'RE CRAZY! WHAT ARE...

SHHH!

WATCH OUT, THE POLICEMAN'S COMING!

HIDE!

28

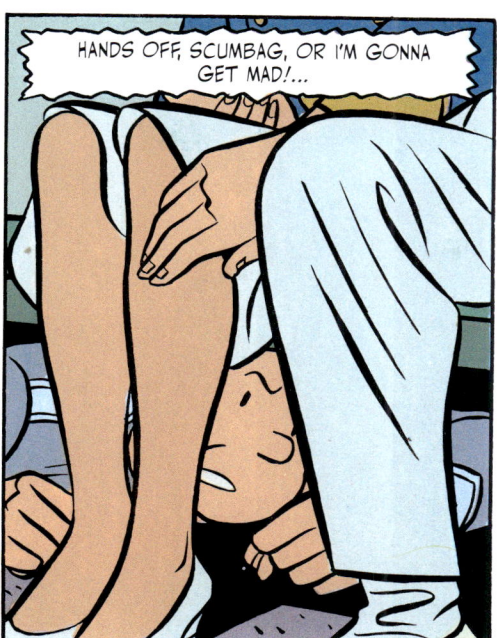

30

THIS PLANE IS REALLY JUST A BIG... TIN CAN.

HA! HA! THAT'S RIGHT AND WE'RE THE CHOPPED MEAT INSIDE!

SUPERLUXE F-52

Menu

Beignets d'Ortolan

Soufflé de caviar à l'oseille

Quenell

SO YOU UNDERSTAND WHAT I WANT YOU TO DO, FREDDY?

SWEEP'S IN JAIL?! THIS IS A DISASTER!

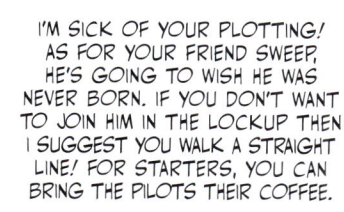

I'M SICK OF YOUR PLOTTING! AS FOR YOUR FRIEND SWEEP, HE'S GOING TO WISH HE WAS NEVER BORN. IF YOU DON'T WANT TO JOIN HIM IN THE LOCKUP THEN I SUGGEST YOU WALK A STRAIGHT LINE! FOR STARTERS, YOU CAN BRING THE PILOTS THEIR COFFEE.

SO I WASN'T HALLUCINATING AFTER ALL. WHEN I CAME BACK TO CABIN 21 FOR THE SECOND TIME, THERE WAS A DIFFERENT LITTLE GIRL IN THERE...

BUT SHE WAS WEARING AN IDENTICAL BLUE DRESS... IF I CAN FIND THE GIRL, THEN THE CREW CAPTAIN WILL HAVE TO LET SWEEP GO!

31

IF I GET CAUGHT... OH! SOMEONE'S COMING...

AHEM...

AHEM...

SOMETHING'S BLOCKING THE DOOR...

?

I WAS BORN IN MONTAUBAN, THE ONLY NORMAL CHILD IN A FAMILY OF SIX MONGOLOIDS. MOM WAS A LITTLE FUNNY IN THE HEAD, AND DAD LOST HIS TO THE GUILLOTINE WITH HIS FRIENDS, THE LAST SURVIVING MEMBERS OF THE BONNOT GANG...

I WAS THE UNUSUAL ONE, SO I GOT LEFT OUT. MY MOTHER GAVE ALL HER LOVE TO MY SIX BROTHERS. EVERY NIGHT MOM WOULD WALK BETWEEN THEIR BEDS, TUCKING THEM IN AND SINGING LULLABIES TO PUT THEM TO SLEEP...

OH! THAT REMINDS ME...

I SHOULD MAKE SURE - GLUG - OUR LITTLE SHEILA'S SLEEPING SOUNDLY.

OOPS, WRONG THING TO SAY...

SO, YOU WERE TALKING ABOUT YOUR MOTHER...

AH YES, MY MOTHER... SHE DIED OF TUBERCULOSIS...BUT I TOOK OVER FOR HER. I DRESSED UP IN A WIG AND A LONG DRESS AND TUCKED MY BROTHERS IN AT NIGHT. IT MADE THE LOSS EASIER FOR THEM...

YIKES!

33

34

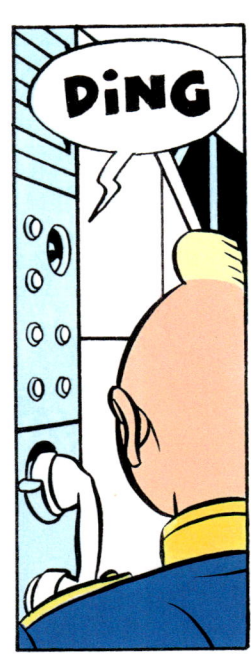

36

DON'T CRY, I'M RIGHT HERE.

SHEILA? DON'T YOU RECOGNIZE ME? I'M YOUR DADDY...

GRETA!

GRETA!

DIRTY SPY! YOU'RE TRYING TO STEAL OUR LITTLE GIRL, TOO!

42

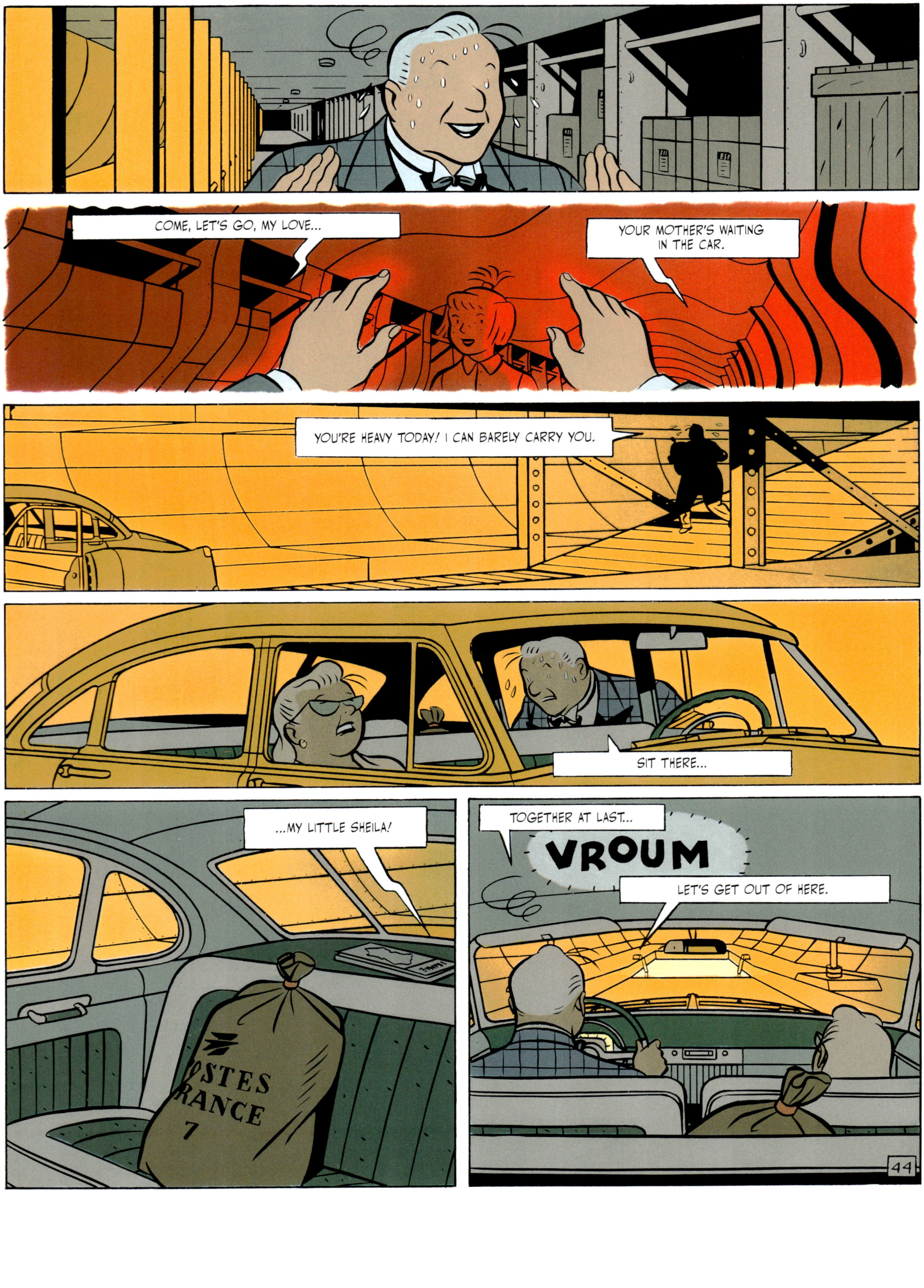

44

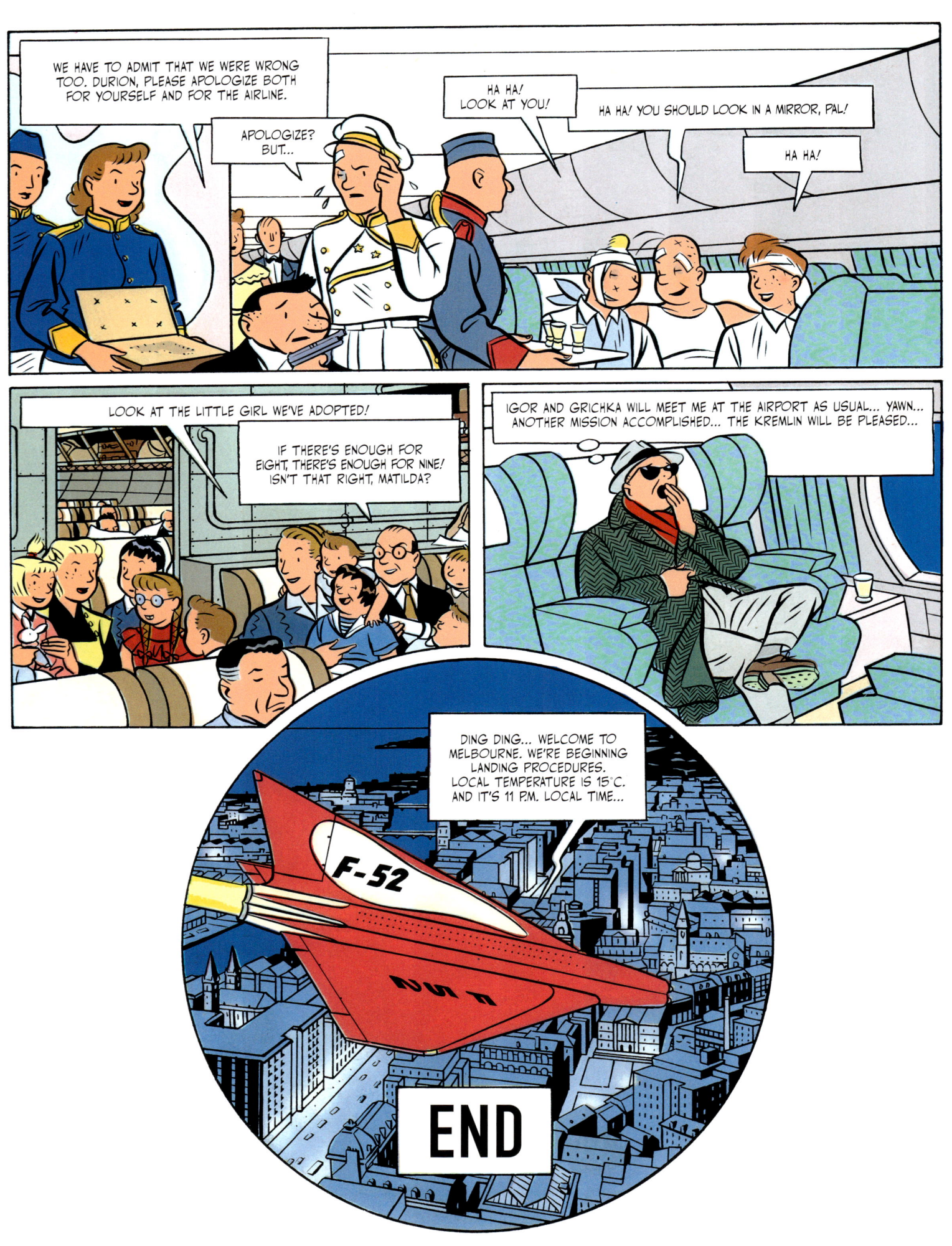

Freddy Lombard

IMAGES AND REGRETS

You're familiar with Belgium, that slightly unreal, somehow timeless country, where things happen that aren't always perfectly clear, and where half the population pretends not to understand the other half when they speak. There's another Belgium, and this one isn't timeless at all. It's located somewhere between 1948 and 1962. Geographically, it can stretch from Budapest to Paris. All is clear, all is logical. We know it's real because we all have a vague memory of having gone there long ago when we were children. This Yves Chaland's Belgium.

Willem
(Chaland Explorer – April, 1990)

He just came to me (...) And since it was an homage to the old Lombard series, I called him Freddy Lombard. The first book was called *"The Will of Godfrey of Bouillon,"* because it took place in Bouillon, in the Belgian Ardennes. I went there to research it. When I got home, I felt so saturated with the atmosphere of the place that I didn't even need to write a script. I just started drawing. I did a page per day. On the 30th page, the end of the story just happened on its own. It was automatic writing from beginning to end.

(*Le Collectionneur de BD* [The Comic collector] – 1992)

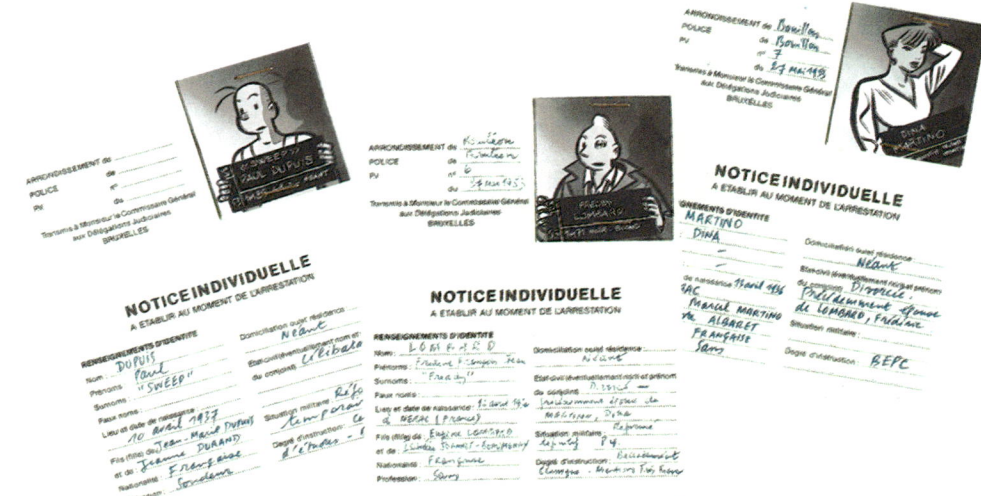

Taken from *"Bouillon police report,"* anthropometrical documents (with photographs and finger prints), 14.5 x 10.5 cm, Magic Strip, 1986.

Freddy Lombard, silkscreen, 60 x 46 cm, Chic Bull editions, 1982.

It's a totally new story starring Godfrey of Bouillon. It takes place partly in the middle ages, partly in our times, thanks to a clever trick… which I'm not going to tell you about.

(*Pour* – February, 1983)

"Het Testament von Godfried Von Bouillon," first edition, in 4 colors, 21.5 x 30.5 cm, Paul Rijperman publisher, 1986.

"Le Testament de Godefroid de Bouillon," first edition (in bi-chrome), 16.5 x 24.9 cm, Magic Strip, 1981.

First draft of page 12 of
"*Le Testament de Godefroid de Bouillon*"
China pen and ink,
23.6 x 33.8 cm, original. 1981.

Frieze taken from "*Le Testament
de Godefroid de Bouillon*"
monochrome color, 3 x 23.2
cm, Magic Strip, 1986.

le testament
Godefro...
de
Bouil...
le

Le testament de Godefroid de Bouillon

· LE JEU ·

Sweep

Morbus

Freddy

Dina

Role playing game box to go with
"Le Testament de Godefroid de Bouillon,"
created by Eric Verhoest,
22 x 29.2 x 3 cm,
Magic Strip, 1989.

42e ANNEE N°16

"MULTI SUNT VOLATI,
PAUCI VERO ELECTI"
(MATTHIEU, XX et XXII)
Aujourd'hui: Saint Donatien
Demain: Sainte Prudence

L'ŒIL DE BOUILLON

LE REGARD DES ARDENNES

29 MAI 1953

ABONNEMENTS

		Belg	Congo	Etrang
1 an...	fr.	330	395	420
6 mois ...		175	205	220
3 mois ...		90	105	115

"Bouillon Royal Police Report"
(six press photos taken from
"The Eye of Bouillon,"
promotional materials,
a restaurant check –
Created by Yann Lepennetier),
Magic Strip, 1986.

I draw the cars and the clothes that I like.
They just happen to be from the 1950's.
I try not to give too many details, not
to make too many specific references in my
stories. The greatest stories take place
in the imaginary, in the marvelous.

(*Le Soir* – December, 1986)

"Le Cimetière des Eléphants,"
cloth bound version,
Les Humanoïdes Associés, 1984.

Image from the title page
from the first printing
Les Humanoïdes Associés, 1984.

"Le Cimetière des Eléphants,"
Eppo #4 cover,
January 28, 1983.

"Freddy et les Collectionneurs,"
Eppo #25 cover,
June 25, 1982.

"Le Cimetière des Eléphants,"
first edition, panel one, page one,
appeared in Eppo, 1982.

"Le Cimetière des Eléphants,"
standard first edition,
Les Humanoïdes Associés, 1984.

Trailer for
"Les Aventures de Freddy Lombard"
in Métal Aventure,
1983, 4-color benday,
21.5 x 28 cm

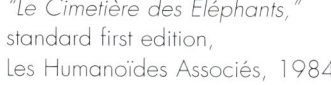

"Le Cimetière des Eléphants,"
first version of panel
seven, page seven and
panel nine, page 11,
appeared in Eppo, 1982.

Freddy Lombard
color poster,
40 x 129 cm,
Les Humanoïdes Associés, 1984.

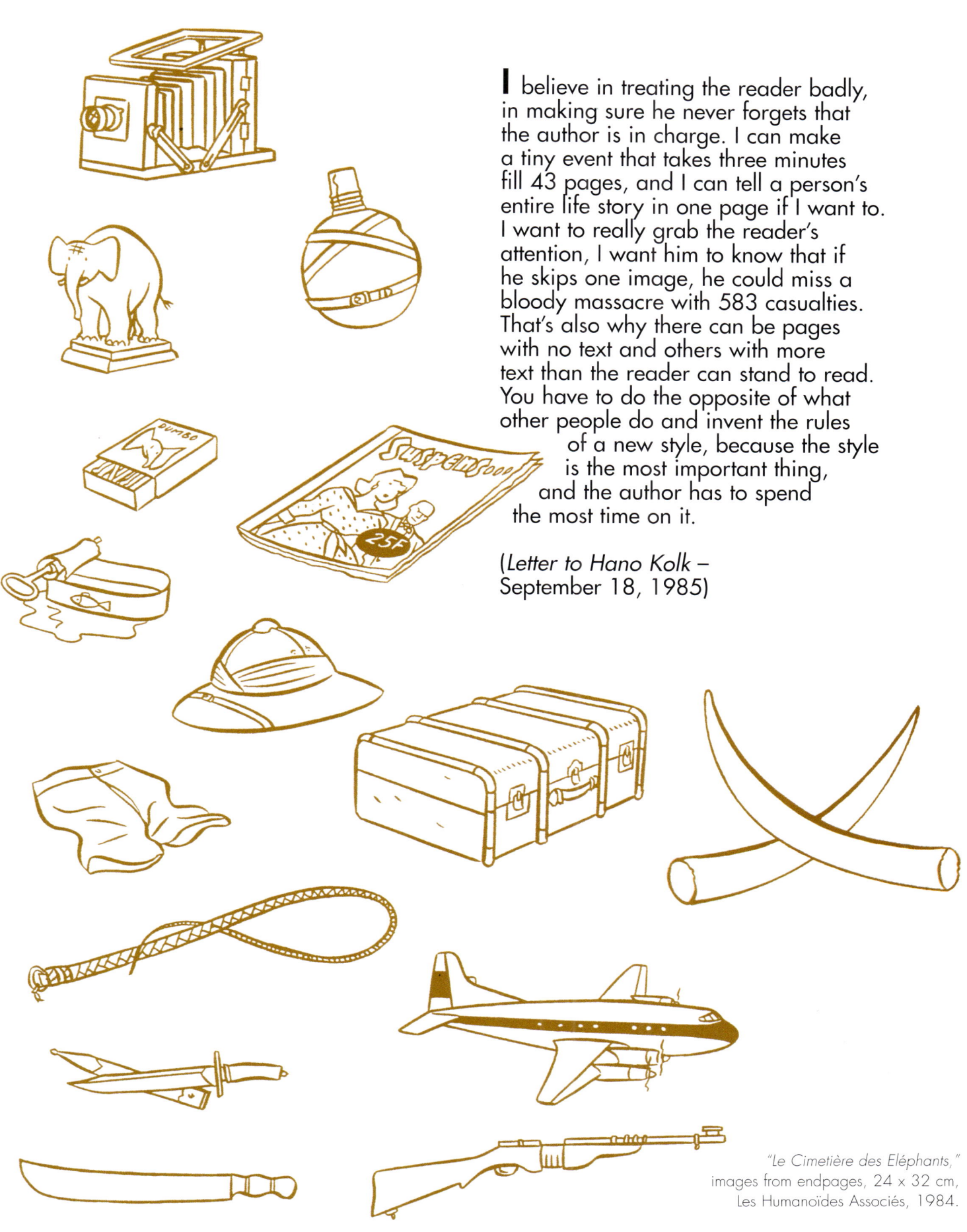

I believe in treating the reader badly, in making sure he never forgets that the author is in charge. I can make a tiny event that takes three minutes fill 43 pages, and I can tell a person's entire life story in one page if I want to. I want to really grab the reader's attention, I want him to know that if he skips one image, he could miss a bloody massacre with 583 casualties. That's also why there can be pages with no text and others with more text than the reader can stand to read. You have to do the opposite of what other people do and invent the rules of a new style, because the style is the most important thing, and the author has to spend the most time on it.

(*Letter to Hano Kolk* – September 18, 1985)

"Le Cimetière des Eléphants," images from endpages, 24 x 32 cm, Les Humanoïdes Associés, 1984.

"Lady Pickpocket,"
two color pages, appeared in Métal Aventure #5, 1984.

Just tell them it's what
the magazines would call
a psychological drama.

(About "La Comète de Carthage" .
Métal Hurlant – July, 1985)

"La Comète de Carthage,"
clothbound version,
Les Humanoïdes Associés, 1986.

Image from the title page
from the first printing
Les Humanoïdes Associés, 1986.

No, I can't tell you who Phidias is, just like I can't tell each of my readers what all the complicated words mean. My readers have to do a little work, and too bad for them if they don't do it. I don't care at all.

(*Leitmotiv* – 1986)

"La Comète de Carthage,"
first version of pages 20 to 23, appeared
in Métal Hurlant #113, 1985.

Like in "*les Pieds-nickeles,*" Freddy, Sweep and Dina have money problems, very concrete problems. I love that. After the war (which is Freddy Lombard's time) there was a glut of heroes who were more worried about getting enough to eat than about chasing outlaws. You'd see them sitting on a public bench, holes in their socks, real down and out types. The war had just ended, it made sense: nobody'd had enough to eat for five years. It's funny and it's a healthy and basic question: what are we having for lunch?

(*PLGPPUR* – March, 1982)

The Gamay wine label,
quadrochrome print,
9.2 x 12.8 cm, heavy paper,
Geneva editors, 1985.

Wine, ocean and comic day:
poster, postcard,
and wine label, 4-color
benday, 9 x 11.6. City of
Cassis editions, April 5, 1986.

"La Comète de Carthage,"
standard edition,
Les Humanoïdes Associés, 1986.

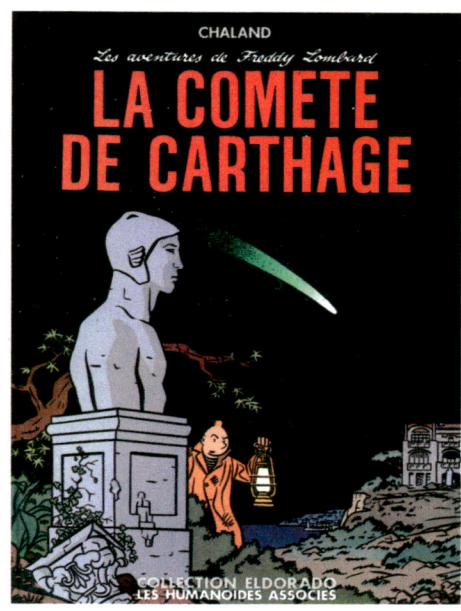

*"**V**acances à Budapest"* came about because I realized that none of the comics from the 50's, Tintin, Spirou etc., had addressed the events in Budapest, the crushing of the rebellion by Russian tanks, even though Hungary is right next door, only 400 kilometers away. Those comics were about current events, but they just never mentioned it. It was a dream subject. I looked back at the comics from the time, and I just felt that this was a book that should have been written back then.

(*Sapristi!* – 1990)

"Vacances à Budapest,"
clothbound version,
Les Humanoïdes Associés, 1988.

Image from the title page
from the first printing
Les Humanoïdes Associés, 1986.

"*Vacances à Budapest,*"
first versions of pages 15, 16, 17 and 18,
China pen and ink,
32.7 x 44 cm, original, 1988.

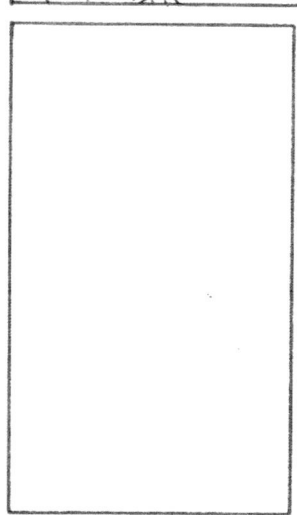

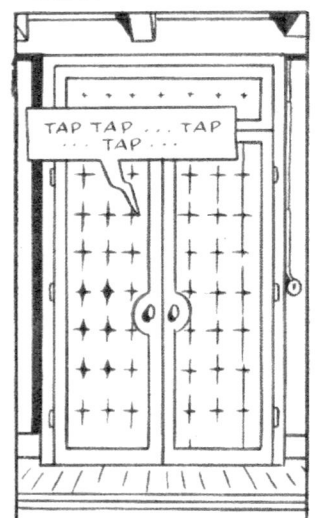

17

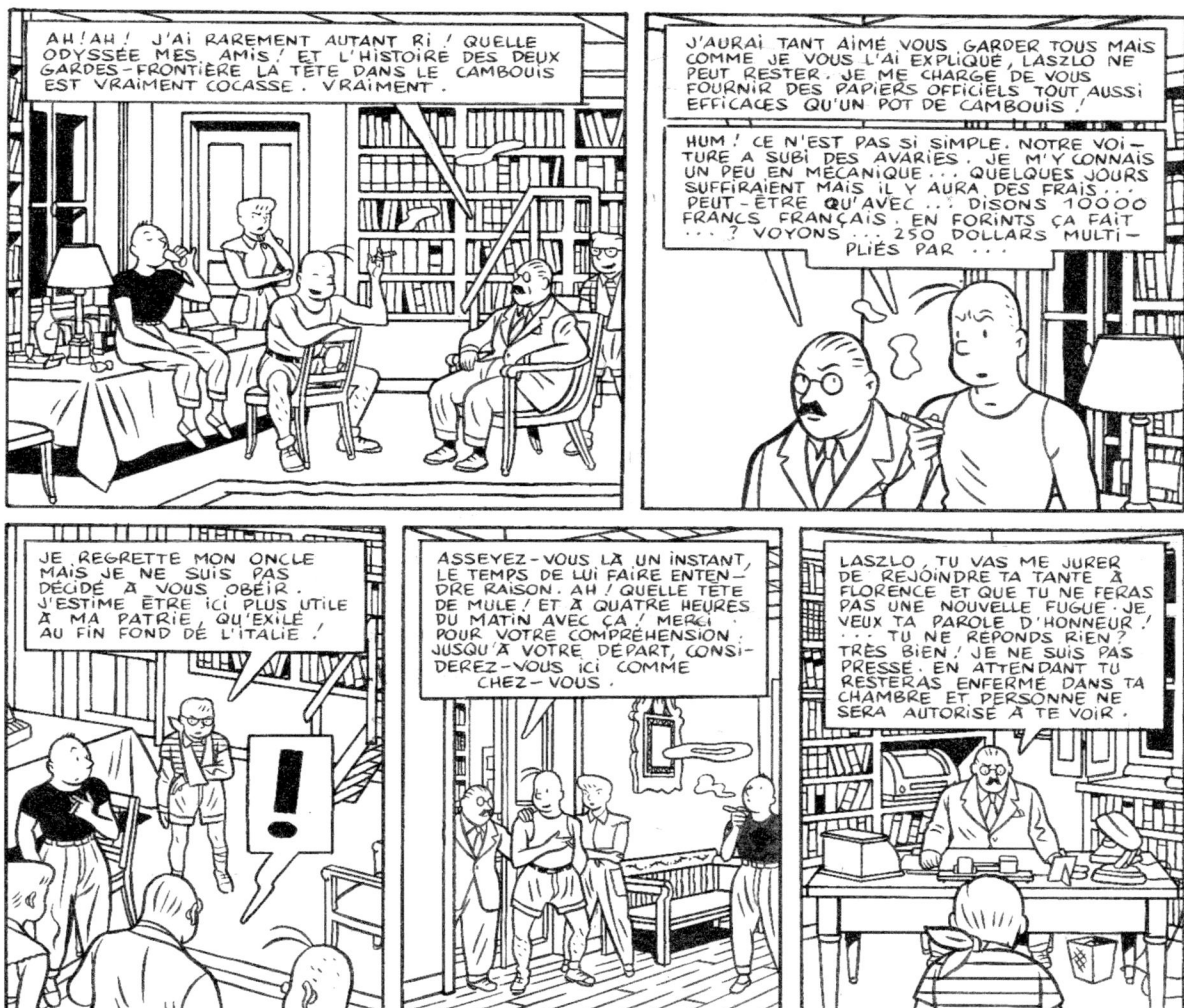

Freddy Lombard's sign would be Aries, the ram. He attacks first, thinks later. Dina is thoughtful and doesn't talk a lot, and Sweep is the strongest of the three. He's big and broad, and he's not too dumb: he bridges the gap between the other two.

(*PLGPPUR* – 1982)

"Vacances à Budapest,"
NKVD stamp used for the freedom papers.
images from endpages,
Les Humanoïdes Associés, 1988.

CHALAND

F-52

LES HUMANOïDES ASSOCIÉS

I got the idea from *"Science and Life"* from the end of the '40s. They'd show pictures of planes like my F-52. They thought planes of the future would be giant, stratospheric and atomic.

(*Le Collectionneur de BD* – 1992)

"F-52," standard edition,
Les Humanoïdes Associés, 1989.

"F-52," first version,
Image from the title page
Les Humanoïdes Associés, 1989.

Comics have never really been a goal for me. Ultimately, my work is my autobiography. I always work with that idea in mind. I love biographies. Beautiful biographies: the obstacles at the beginning, bitter work in a miserable attic room, then the revolutionary discovery, but the story gets complicated: people turn against the creative genius. What will happen?

(*PLGPPUR* – 1982)

"F-52" page 43,
first version, 24 x 32 cm,
China pen and ink,
original, 1988.